"An honest depiction of how [Hilarie] transformed from actress to farmer, reconnecting to the land she grew up on while navigating motherhood."
—*Marie Claire*

"In her new memoir, Hilarie candidly speaks about love, life, careers, and everything in between."
—*People* magazine

"Hilarie's warmth and humor are on full display. *The Rural Diaries* reads like a favorite girls' night chat."
—*Country Living*

"This funny, insightful look at Hilarie's time on her family's farm is a must read."
—*Town & Country*

"Hilarie's charisma and charm can be enjoyed in *The Rural Diaries*, which tells the heart-warming story of looking for her place in the world."
—*Refinery29*

"*The Rural Diaries* reads like a favorite girls' night chat." —*Country Living*

The Rural Diaries

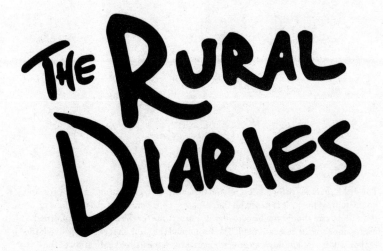

THE RURAL DIARIES

Love, Livestock, and

Big Life Lessons

Down on Mischief Farm

Hilarie Burton Morgan

HarperOne

An Imprint of HarperCollinsPublishers

This book includes information related to health, diet, gardening, agriculture, and home improvement. It is based on the research, experience and observations of the author, and should not be considered a substitute for the advice of a qualified professional in the relevant field. The author and the publisher expressly disclaim responsibility for any adverse effects arising from the use or application of the information contained herein.

Quote on page 5 attributed to Robert Louis Stevenson comes from the subtitle of the play *Admiral Guinea*.

Quote from page 39 attributed to L. M. Montgomery comes from a TV series adaptation of Montgomery's books.

Quote on page 193 attributed to Gabriel García Márquez comes from the book *Living to Tell the Tale*.

THE RURAL DIARIES. Copyright © 2020 by North Ithaca, Inc. All rights reserved. Printed in the United States of America. No part of this book may be used or reproduced in any manner whatsoever without written permission except in the case of brief quotations embodied in critical articles and reviews. For information, address HarperCollins Publishers, 195 Broadway, New York, NY 10007.

HarperCollins books may be purchased for educational, business, or sales promotional use. For information, please email the Special Markets Department at SPsales@harpercollins.com.

FIRST HARPERCOLLINS PAPERBACK EDITION PUBLISHED IN 2021

Designed by SBI Book Arts, LLC
Dandelion illustration by Epine/Shutterstock

Library of Congress Cataloging-in-Publication Data is available upon request.

ISBN 978-0-06-286271-6

21 22 23 24 25   LSC   10 9 8 7 6 5 4 3 2 1

To my Jeffrey.
You turned every daydream into a reality. I love you.

And to Gus and George.
I wanted you my whole life and I'm so glad you're mine.

CONTENTS

PREFACE

Dear Diary,

Last weekend, Jeffrey and I got married. Really and truly married. It was the culmination of a decade of partnership, trial and error, and most importantly, effort. For years we had called each other "husband" and "wife." We lived like we were married, raised our kids as a unit, built homes and a future together. But we knew that we'd sidestepped that very real rite of passage.

It was fine. Livable. Happy. But our life at Mischief Farm demanded better of us. We'd found a sanctuary where authenticity mattered. The truths at the farm were concrete. The fields had to be mowed. The wood had to be chopped. The gardens had to be weeded. And the animals had to be fed. We wanted to be one of those truths.

So, on a bright, blue-skied October afternoon—very much like the day we first laid eyes on Mischief Farm, with the kaleidoscope of hues that autumn brings—we exchanged vows in front of a colorful collection of characters from our life. We chose the Bowery Hotel, a standard haunt of ours, as we were drawn to the history and mischief of the neighborhood. The Bowery is the oldest road in New York City, from the Dutch word *bouwerij*, meaning farm. All roads lead back to the farm.

I feel strong. When we made the choice to cast off the skin of our former lives, it was with tremendous uncertainty. We barely knew each other. But this place and this life were worth the risk.

They were worth the hardships we faced. They were worth every effort. Our wedding wasn't the beginning of a life together. It was a celebration and a thank-you to the people and places that shaped our past ten years.

Love is like farm work. It requires consistency, and imagination. Your body will ache and you will be fatigued, but there is no greater reward than seeing the fruits of your labor.

In a parting gift to our guests, I included packets of Mischief Farm Marigolds, seeds I'd sown from my own gardens. I hope they go out there in the world and grow and bloom and multiply with all the love from which they sprang.

Hilarie Burton Morgan
10.13.19

PROLOGUE

"What kind of farm did you grow up on?" Folks always throw that question at me any time they find out about Mischief Farm. *Oh you know, the lower-middle-class kind, which grows swing sets and grubby children and is surrounded by a chain-link fence.* My childhood was fantastically suburban. Before Mischief Farm, the only farming I had done had been through literary adventuring. Green Gables. *Little House on the Prairie.* I longed for the landscape of *Wuthering Heights.* Hell, even *Animal Farm* held a certain appeal.

Both of my parents had agricultural experience, though. Their stories were fables in our family. My father didn't wax poetic about his childhood of manual labor. His tales were more cautionary. We never ate lamb, because his family had kept sheep for a while. It scarred him. Then there were the years they dealt in chickens. Equally scarring. Eggs must be scrambled to ultimate tightness, and any meat is to be cooked about four levels past well done. Hell or high water, we were gonna be spared from any barnyard diseases. It was clear that farming was not a pleasurable career path for my father's family. Just a way to scrape by and keep seven hungry kids fed.

My mother, on the other hand, comes from real-deal farmers in Iowa. Multigenerational corn and soybean and pig farmers with huge tracts of land. The first time I visited my great aunt's house on the farm in Iowa, I found it exotic. They had a hammock at the edge of a cornfield, and a dozen barn cats skittered around. My three brothers chased the cats against the backdrop of sunset, and I grabbed one of the kittens and settled into the hammock. Looking out on the cornfield, I marveled that this is what they woke up to every day. Even when I was a kid dreaming of being a showbiz dame like Doris Day or Debbie Reynolds or Katharine Hepburn, I held on to this vision of farm life.

I grew up in the little town of Sterling Park, Virginia, population nine thousand. I kept the pace of the Blue Ridge Mountains. I could hear cows lowing from my high school. It was a pastoral community. And then Amazon opened a huge headquarters in Northern Virginia, right in my little town, and suddenly an influx of two hundred thousand people completely erased the childhood that I had grown up with.

Jeffrey grew up in Kirkland, Washington. Once upon a time it was a tiny waterfront suburb of Seattle. He camped with the Boy Scouts, rode a mean old pony named Brownie at his grandma's pig farm, and played in the woods and water of the Pacific Northwest. Then, Boeing visited, saw lots of space and a good quality of life, moved in, and erased those things. So with both of our childhood communities swallowed up by big business, he and I never had the luxury of that fairy tale of raising kids in our hometowns.

Randomly, we found a new hometown: Rhinebeck, New York. A place that felt like we'd known it all along. We marveled that a village like this still existed. So we were aware that when you find a community that nurtures you and your family, it isn't enough to just live in it; you must also nurture and protect that place and all the people who give you respite, solace, joy, and just enough hell to keep life interesting.

So, folks, this is a love letter. To a town. To a farm. To a man.

Part One

PLANT

1

Don't judge each day by the harvest you
reap but by the seeds that you plant.

—**Robert Louis Stevenson**

The first time we drove into Rhinebeck, I knew I'd found
a place I belonged. As we crossed the Kingston Bridge, the
world cracked open before us, all sun and sky and river.
A large billboard for the Dutchess County Fair promised livestock and carnival rides and country music acts. A driftwood
sculpture that loosely resembled a dinosaur peeped out from behind a few trees as we approached the town. I scratched the hair
at the base of Jeff's skull and kept my hand on his neck. It felt
bold. Together for fewer than two years, we hadn't exactly been
in a honeymoon phase. Parenting was hard. Being apart for work
was hard. Not having a real place to call home was hard. But riding along side by side, we felt light and hopeful and new. Our five-
month-old son, Gus, babbled in his car seat. This felt like a place
where things were made. A place that invited possibility.

We rolled through Rhinebeck Village, a tiny Dutch community that reminded me of Pella, Iowa, where my mom's family was
from—skinny buildings stacked up against each other that housed

long-established mom-and-pop shops where you went just as much for the camaraderie as for any material goods.

Rhinebeck has only two commercial streets: Route 9, or Mill Street, which has a couple of churches, a post office, and a bank, and Market Street. On the corner stands a handsome brick building with a sign that reads Rhinebeck Department Store. At the crossroads is the Beekman Arms, a stately white inn with black trim and American flags snapping in the breeze. It's the oldest operating inn in the country. George Washington and other revolutionaries stayed there, and the Fourth Regiment of the Continental Army practiced drills on its lawn.

We parked and asked a couple of people where to get a cup of coffee, and they directed us to the candy store on Market Street. We passed one cute painted storefront after another, noticing how the sidewalk was hemmed in by a tidy line of trees whose trunks were surrounded by bursts of colorful flowers. Small crowds of smiling people moved along to a seemingly well-rehearsed choreography: nod, smile, wave at the baby, tip the hat, smile again. Like out of an old musical, the town had a rhythm that made it feel like someone might burst into song at any moment.

At the end of the block, we stepped inside the candy store, a tiny jewel box of a shop, cool and dark and soothing. The shelves were lined with luminescent rows of penny candy. I spotted Cow Tales, which I hadn't eaten since I was twelve.

A flushed, smiling gentleman with a bush of curly hair chatted easily as he rang us up. "Welcome to town. What brings you guys here?"

"Oh, we're looking at a house," Jeff replied.

The man was incandescent. "You guys are gonna love it here. You're just gonna love it. I moved up from the city too."

We smiled and thanked him for the coffee, and Jeff patted my rear on the way out the door. He gets handsy when he's excited. Though I didn't quite know how yet, I sensed our lives were about to change.

Of all the twists and turns a life takes, driving into Rhinebeck was one of the few turns when I felt truly home. But to make sense of how we got here, I have to back up for a moment and point out the seeds of change that led me here.

Seed One: Loss

The trajectory of my life changed in 2007. At the time, I was working on *One Tree Hill* and feeling a bit lost. I worked hard all day, then went out and sang karaoke in bars with my friends till closing, then got up early the next day and worked again. And while I was smiling and perfecting my rendition of Dolly Parton's "Applejack," I was a miserable girl. My whole life had been an ambitious climb to become a working actor. And I'd done it. So why was I so damn disappointed?

In August, we were shooting a scene down by Cape Fear River. It was one of those big days, with every actor in every scene and a hundred extras. Overwhelmed, I retreated to the air conditioning of my trailer and scrolled through MySpace alerts on my phone.

A buddy from high school—Stan—popped up in my messages. I don't remember the exact message, but I have a vague recollection of his trying to gently break the news to me. "Hilarie . . . I know it's been a long time . . . not sure if anyone else has reached out . . . I know you guys were close . . ."

Then he said it. Scott Kirkpatrick had died in Iraq.

My heart skittered in my chest.

In high school, Scott and Stan had been part of the cool, drama-goth-poetry slam circle that I idolized. Scott was two years older than me, and I wanted to do everything just like him, including writing and acting.

Scott and his friends would pick me up after the football games I cheered at, and we'd drive to Clyde's in Reston, where we'd order a bucket of sweet potato fries and they'd smoke clove cigarettes. We'd work on our tortured poems and go to poetry slams together—me in my cheerleading uniform and them in their big dark trench coats and little Dracula glasses. Scott was the kind of person who made you feel like big, magical things were right around the corner, and you just had to be bold enough to make the turn. We all followed, dutifully.

After graduation, Scott, with his Kurt Cobain hair and lanky gait, became a nationally ranked slam poet and traveled all over the country. Then, after September 11, he joined the army. When I heard the news, I was shocked.

Scott deployed to Iraq and became a sergeant, then got married and was planning to leave the army and come home to his wife. He and I kept in touch via MySpace, where he gave me hell for being on the cover of *Maxim* with all the girls from *One Tree Hill*. "What the fuck's going on Burton? That's not the girl I know."

We'd made plans to return to our theater roots and make indie movies together once he got out of the service. The big plan was to do an update of a play we'd done in high school—Dostoyevsky's *The Idiot*. I'd begun mapping the story out, filling a spiral notebook with ideas and research.

He was almost done with his tour when somebody shot one of the guys in his squad. Scott and another soldier chased the attacker into a building that had been rigged to explode.

This was a cheat that I couldn't stand for. Not Scott.

My life took a turn, and I struggled with the grief and unfairness of losing him, his friendship, and the future we had plotted.

I wrangled one day off of work to attend Scott's funeral at Arlington Cemetery. With its meticulous grounds and stark white headstones set with eerie geometry, it is both one of the most beautiful places I've seen in the world and a museum of sadness. A crowd flocked into the chapel, packed tight in the sweltering August heat, dizzy with grief. Scott was eulogized by a higher-up in the army and awarded several honors for his bravery. I grew anxious as the service neared its end; I did not want them to stop talking about my friend.

We were ushered outside to take part in the procession to Scott's final resting place. Goths and generals side by side. It was a weird, mournful military pageant that Scott would have appreciated.

At his gravesite they played taps, and each note was agony. *Don't end. Don't end. Don't end*, I thought, not wanting to get back in the car and go on as if everything were normal.

After the funeral, friends and family were invited to Scott's parents' place. In the years since we had graduated they'd moved to a little farm. The house had a wide front porch, and there were goats and sheep, and a handsome tractor was prominently displayed. They called it Whack-a-Mole Farm. I didn't want to leave.

Scott's death snapped my priorities and goals back into focus. I had spent the previous few years wandering, never really finding my place, but I wanted more. I wanted a family. I wanted a home that could be a refuge and a blank canvas that would allow me to daydream, to take risks, to try and fail and try again. I wanted to push myself every day. I wanted to make every moment intentional. Wake up intentionally. Work intentionally. Eat intentionally. And rest intentionally.

It was time to make a change, so I left *One Tree Hill.* I'd always wanted to travel and to write, so I started to work on a novel, bought a one-way ticket to Paris, and rented an apartment across from Notre Dame Cathedral.

Before I flew across the Atlantic, I took what I thought would be one last trip to Los Angeles for a few days. I had a handful of meetings, and I wanted to see my friends Jensen and Danneel (our friendship was one of the best things to come from working on *One Tree Hill*). I'd often slept on their couch, and they listened to me lament about shitty boyfriends and feeling adrift in life. Those two are so damn generous and meddling, so naturally, when I got to LA, they wanted to set me up with a friend of theirs—but they wouldn't tell me who.

Seed Two: Mr. Morgan

I watched from across the bar as a man dressed all in leather sauntered through the front door. Surely this wasn't the friend

Danneel and Jensen had in mind? Motorcycle helmet in hand, the man hugged them and made very direct eye contact with me as he shook my hand. "I'm Jeffrey." He had bracelets stacked to his elbows and large silver rings on damn near every finger. I leaned in to Danneel, "Good lord, D. You invited a midlife crisis to dinner!"

Hours later, we closed down that little Irish pub, and then all four of us ended up back at Jeffrey Dean Morgan's house. He had just bought a huge, beautiful place in Studio City, a Mediterranean beast of a home that had more than five thousand square feet and was the exact opposite of the intimate (and haunted) Victorian I was living in, in Wilmington, North Carolina.

As we entered the house, a dignified lady Rottweiler mix with soulful eyes met me. "This is Bisou," Jeff said as I scratched the fur behind Bisou's ears. She pressed into me and Jeff smiled. "She usually doesn't like other girls." Apparently, Bisou had been less than fond of some of his exes.

"Looks like I'm not like other girls."

Jeff gave us a tour, and when I saw the comedically stereotypical bachelor-pad sheepskin fur on his bed, I rolled my eyes. He swore up and down that it was for Bisou. I believed him, though I didn't let him know that. I'd seen his Harley, but I also had seen his car as we walked through the garage, a "dad car," with room for baby seats and dogs and groceries. I was surprised to realize that he hadn't bought the single-guy party house; he had bought the family home, with bedrooms for kids and a big yard with a lemon tree. As I said goodbye to Jeff that night, I could feel myself becoming more intrigued.

A few hours after we'd said goodbye, I flew back to Wilmington. Two days later my doorbell rang. A package sat outside, with blocky, masculine handwriting on the FedEx shipping label. No way.

I tore off the seal and out tumbled guidebooks on Paris, Raymond Carver anthologies, and a beautiful, red, leather-bound journal, which Jeffrey had inscribed: "Go nuts. Xoxo jdm, Miss your face."

There was also a note that read, "For someone I just met, I can't stop thinking about you."

Seed Three: The Land of Enchantment

A day later Jeffrey called. "I've bought you a plane ticket from Wilmington to New Mexico. I want to take you on a date. This weekend. I packed a suit."

It was romantic as hell, but my heart dropped into my belly. I was supposed to be leaving for my new life in Paris, not getting tangled up with a leather-wearing, motorcycle-riding, Raymond-Carver-book-sending guy.

Fuck it. I thought. *What's the worst that could happen?*

In the days leading up to our first date, we had long, rambling phone calls that lasted until sunrise. I shared so many personal details with him, including the Native American family history I had been uncovering. So when I arrived in New Mexico, Jeffrey didn't present me with flowers, wine, or chocolates. He gave me a tacked wood quirt with long leather straps, half battle club, half riding whip.

Standing in the living room of his little rental house running my fingers over it, I felt so known. Tears stung my eyes, and I tried hard not to cry.

I had made all these plans—I had written a quarter of my novel

and rented the place in Paris—and here was this curveball changing the whole game. Jeffrey was so sure of himself, so sure of me,
and so sure that the two of us were going to be together.

I was terrified.

Right away we began negotiating the terms of our new life together, meandering behind a mariachi band as it led a wedding
parade through the Santa Fe town square. Passing a tiny art gallery,
he peeped in the windows. "We're gonna have a shop like this."

"How many kids are we having?" I asked.

"Two. Three?" That worked for me. I smiled at him.

"You gonna be good cop or bad cop?" he asked.

"Oh bad cop, for sure."

Relieved, he added, "When we get our ranch, we'll get you some
of those buffalo you're so excited about. Let them just roam and
take over the place. Dot and Kenny."

"Okay, so, kids. Ranch. Buffalo. All sounds good."

"What do you want?" he asked.

"Don't laugh. But I've always wanted a Christmas tree farm."

I braced myself for the knee jerk "you dork" reaction that always
came when I told people about my Christmas tree farm dream.
Two months into my run as a VJ on MTV's *TRL*, the Offspring
(don't pretend you didn't sing along to the massively inappropriate
"Pretty Fly [For a White Guy]") announced that they were going
to give away a *million dollars* as a promotion for their new album
Conspiracy of One. Kirsten Dunst was our guest. Like me, she had
recently enrolled in college.

Carson Daly asked her, "What would you do with the money?"

"Get flip-flops for the showers in the dorm!" The audience
roared at her hilarious answer.

"What about you, Hil? One million dollars. What do you buy?"

"Oh, no question: a Christmas tree farm!"

Crickets.

"Huh. Okay then." Carson pivoted and sent us into a commercial break. My segment producer pulled me backstage. "You can't say stuff like that. It's not cool."

Cool or not, the thing was, I really did want that Christmas tree farm. When I was growing up in Northern Virginia, the most magical place in the whole wide world was Reston Farm Market. It was more than fifteen acres of gardens, new plants in the spring, pumpkins in October, and at Christmas, it glistened with twinkly lights, bonfires, and real magic. Out front was an old wagon piled with brightly wrapped presents, and just outside the door were great mounds of Christmas trees. It also was next door to a petting zoo, which for a long time while I was in elementary school had a buffalo, hence my obsession with them.

Outside, chestnuts were roasting and the air smelled of pine and earth and freshly ground coffee. Inside the old converted barn was a holiday emporium. The tables held fresh eggs in baskets, crates of apples, and seasonal treats from pickles to smoked trout. Rainbows of hand-dipped candles hung from the rafters, and there were wreaths made from dried corn or pinecones, garlands, dried flowers, jams and butters, and hand-stitched, hand-knitted, hand-carved, and hand-painted *everything*, from Christmas ornaments to tablecloths. An enormous trimmed tree gleamed in the middle of the room, and Mrs. Claus was always nestled in a rocker, reading books to us kids after we'd sat on Santa's knee and told him what we most wanted.

All my Christmasy, folksy dreams began there at Reston Farm

Market, and I harbored a fantasy that after my acting career, I would build my own version of it. I wanted a place where families could come together and make holiday traditions—Christmas caroling, Easter egg hunts—or other traditions, like drive-in movies during the summer. It would be a place for people to make memories.

I felt a little closer to that dream when Jeffrey said, "I love Christmas trees. I put Christmas lights on everything." There had, in fact, been Christmas lights on that lemon tree in his backyard in LA. "How many acres?"

"A hundred?"

"A hundred acres works."

Seed Four: Rolling the Dice

Reader, I didn't go to Paris.

The plan had been to make a new start and find something that was mine. As it turns out, I found that thing a hell of a lot more quickly than I'd expected.

Jeffrey and I weren't made for dating. He was the man I was gonna get old and boring with. Instead of late nights out at clubs or wining and dining, at night we'd settle in and watch an episode of *Lonesome Dove*. We decided that when we had a kid, we'd name him Gus, after Robert Duvall's character. Who *doesn't* see that prostitute-loving cowboy and think, "I'm gonna name my baby after that ol' cuss!"?

As the credits rolled, Jeffrey turned to me and asked, "Do you just want to do this? Do you want to try and have a family?" We'd known each other for less than a month.

Doctors had told me that I was going to have a lot of trouble having kids because I'd always had what was referred to as "girl problems." I had never had a period until my doctor put me on birth control pills when I was eighteen. I didn't have an eating disorder or any illness; I was just a really, really, really late bloomer.

I told Jeffrey, "This is going to be difficult." He wasn't concerned, so we took all the fences down.

When I got my period in June, I stood in the kitchen and cried. I could see the next ten years unfolding. I could see how every month we'd be disappointed. Then it would become a sensitive subject. Then it would become a fight. Then it would break us. I saw all the bad spooling out before me.

But Jeff just stood beside me and listened as all my fear poured out. Then he turned to me and said very matter-of-factly, "Hilarie, it's been a month. I don't think you understand that this is going to happen."

The next month I found out I was pregnant.

Seed Five: Lost Angeles

LA was Jeff's turf. I'd only ever visited the city, though when I was a child I was obsessed with it. There is a rather embarrassing video of seven- or eight-year-old me one Easter morning. My parents are asking me, "Where do you live, Hilarie?" And in this over-the-top Katharine Hepburn voice I announce, "I live on Hollywood Boulevard and I have palm trees in my front yard." The summer after eighth grade my dad had a business meeting in California, and rather than fly, he drove the family across country. My folks took me to Graceland because I was fanatical about Elvis. We stopped along the way and saw buffalo. Then, right before we got to LA, we stopped at a gas station where I saw my first palm tree. I cried. Then, tears rolling down my cheeks, I hugged the tree, and my parents snapped a picture.

Even though I had wanted to live in LA so desperately, my years working in television had soured me on the city. My baby was gonna be born in North Carolina, surrounded by family and friends. My brother and Nick, my bestie and writing partner, threw me a big baby shower in Wilmington, and all the crew from *One Tree Hill* showed up with their favorite books for my boy.

But then, in a last-minute change of plans, Jeffrey and I decided to have the baby in California. Jeffrey had gotten a job he really, *really* wanted. So dammit—I was gonna be a team player. On Valentine's Day, eight months pregnant, I got on a plane and moved myself and all of our baby's books and hand-sewn crib bumpers to Los Angeles.

I googled "midwives" there and found Deborah Frank. Waddling into her office three weeks away from giving birth, I thanked her over and over again for seeing me and said, "Hey, I don't have anybody. Can you please be my midwife?"

She looked me in the eye, emanating a warmth that made me feel like everything would work out. "I'll help you."

The week Gus was due Jeff had to go to Texas. It was just a quick trip to shadow a detective down there, and after a week spent visiting morgues and crime scenes, he came home exhausted and emotionally drained. Dead bodies will do that to you.

Understandably, Jeff passed out early that first night home, so I called my high school best friend, Sarah Barnes. We'd gotten pregnant within months of each other. I sat in the rocking chair in the nursery I'd decorated, so lonely and scared. Of my friends,

Sarah has always been the sassiest, and pregnancy had made her only punchier. We cackled into the wee hours, until my sides began to cramp with laughter. "Stop!" I told her. "I feel sick." We hung up and I sent her a picture of my beached-whale belly. *I think that jerk just put me into labor,* I thought. When I woke a few hours later at 5 o'clock in the morning, I was having contractions every eight minutes.

Jeffrey was sleeping soundly, so I snuck into a little office he had upstairs and called Deborah. She spoke in her soft, calm voice and, as if women had babies every day (which, for her, they did), simply said, "Okay, I'm going on a hike. Drink a glass of wine in the bathtub, and I'll be over as soon as I'm done."

It seemed a strange thing to tell a pregnant lady to do, but I followed directions and poured a glass of red wine, lowering myself very carefully into the tub. I expected all my pain and worries to melt away and to find serenity. Wrong. Now I was just wet and uncomfortable and maybe tipsy. Not a good look. Jeffrey came into the bathroom bleary-eyed and too tired to keep the judgment out of his voice, "What are you doing? You're drinking?"

"Jeffrey, I finally got permission after nine months. I'm going for it."

Deborah came over at 9 a.m. and checked me; I was only two centimeters dilated. "It's going to be a while. We'll probably go to the hospital tonight." Then she left.

I was disappointed. It was *really* starting to hurt, and I couldn't imagine this going on all day long. My parents arrived, having caught multiple connecting flights from North Carolina. They were exhausted and confused, since I wasn't due for a few more days. I hunched over the couch armrest trying to remain chipper through the contractions.

"Hi Mommy. Dad. I'd hug you, but . . ." Ugh. The air was knocked out of my lungs. They'd been at the house for maybe half an hour when my mom looked at me and said, "I get that you have a high threshold for pain. But this is . . . a lot. Call the midwife."

Deborah came back over and, surprise, surprise—I was at seven centimeters. "We gotta go!" she called out to the house.

Jeff drove us to the hospital, flying over Laurel Canyon, which is a road straight out of a ten-year-old boy's video game. If you're in the trenches of labor, it's a particularly nauseating road to be on.

Led Zeppelin's "Immigrant Song" came on, and my contractions were timing out perfectly to it. I was punching the ceiling of Jeff's car and howling along with the "Ahhaa ah—AH!" of Robert Plant, while my poor mother was saying in the backseat, "This is so baaaad."

Seed Six: My Boy

Our labor and delivery room was busy. Deborah was calm and assertive, suggesting that Jeff and I duck into the little bathroom attached to the delivery room. Perhaps a shower with warm water on my back would help ease some of the pain.

See, I had decided early on that I was going drug-free. If you want the drugs, get all the drugs, sweetheart. No judgment here. But for me, I felt like I had something to prove. I'd felt weak and dumb and small my whole pregnancy. My whole adult life, really. There was so much I was unsure of. But in all my prep work I was sure of one thing: since the dawn of time, women have been having babies. Women are strong and majestic and powerful enough to create other human beings. And I was going to prove to myself, and to everyone else on the planet, that I was a sturdy, badass woman.

That's all well and good—until you're at nine centimeters. I stood in the shower as Jeff fed me popsicles, looking very LA in his torn-up jeans, boots, and black T-shirt and all his Chrome Hearts jewelry. (My parents used to call him a fortune teller and asked whether he would read their palms. He was very insulted.)

The contractions were fast, and I was scared, making very un-ladylike baritone groans. Jeff tried harmonizing with my noise, which made me laugh, which made the contractions hurt more, which made me moan louder. My mother was eyeballing everything, wondering who her daughter had taken up with. My father was out in the waiting room befriending an Indian family who pulled beautiful china, crystal glasses, and a feast out of picnic baskets while they waited for their family member's birth.

During a lull in the contractions, Jeff took my hand and bent low toward my ear, "Hil, you mind if I go smoke real fast? This is kind of really stressful."

"Yes," I whispered.

"Yes? You mind?" He wasn't sure he heard me correctly.

I was direct. "Yes." I think he underestimated how aggressive our son was being. In fact, no one seemed to understand that this baby was *coming*.

I moved to the bed, and a perfectly nice nurse who gave zero shits about my labor shuffled in and out, filling out paperwork and dealing with all the minutia of childbirth. All I wanted in the whole world was for her to hold my foot so I could bear down during contractions. But it was like trying to herd a cat. The plan had been for Jeffrey to stand up beside my head and not see anything. I was supposed to catch the baby.

"You're doing great Hilarie," Deborah said. "I can see the baby's head. When you feel the next contraction, bear down."

For a moment, I wondered whether I could call the whole thing off and go to sleep. I just wanted to rest. I didn't think I could push again. But my body had its own ideas. My muscles tightened in anticipation, and I felt a big contraction build—but the nurse had disappeared.

"Somebody help me!" I cried. My poor mother already was giving me her arm to grab onto for support, cursing in my ear like a high school football coach: "You got this, dammit. Just focus. You fucking got this." (This memory still makes me laugh.)

"I messed up," I moaned. "Can I get drugs?"

"You're fine," Deborah reminded me in her sweet, holistic voice. And in some instinctual way, this woman whom I had known for only a few brief appointments read me like a book and said just the thing to get me focused: "I have very high expectations for you Hilarie. You are going to do a wonderful job today."

Well that was it. Now I'd been challenged. Forget the nurse who kept wandering off. "Jeffrey, will you hold my foot?" I asked him. Poor buddy wasn't ready for that assignment, but to his credit, he stepped up.

Another contraction rocked through me, and Jeffrey was right down where the action was.

The last ten minutes were pure hell.

Then Deborah said, "Now. This is going to be the last one. Do you want to catch the baby?"

But I was so exhausted. "No, no. I can't."

"Who do you want to catch the baby?"

"Jeff will do it," I managed to say.

Then this man who had been looking at bodies in a morgue all week went pale and glassy-eyed. "I will?" Quickly, he adjusted. "Sure I will."

The final contraction broke, and Jeffrey was the first person to lay hands on Gus.

He raised our boy up and laid his squirmy little body on my chest. Jeffrey and I were bound forever in that moment. Then Deborah busied Jeff with the task of cutting the umbilical cord. All the while this magical little stranger—my Gus—rooted around, found me, and started nursing. Just like that, there was my baby.

Gus didn't look anything like the person I had had in my mind for the past almost ten months. Instead, he looked just like Jeff. He had his dad's strong nose and a very prominent chin dimple that was most certainly not mine. He was a very furry little baby. He had hair that came down to his eyebrows, furry shoulder blades, and a double row of eyelashes. I couldn't take my eyes off him. He was a love that I knew. He knew my heartbeat. He knew me inside and out. He was perfect.

Jeff leaned down and whispered in my ear, "I'm so proud of you."

2

We are homesick most for the places
we have never known.

—Carson McCullers,
The Heart Is a Lonely Hunter

I was obsessed with Gus. Your whole life, you're hunting for
the perfect person to sweep you off your feet and make all
your days magical. My perfect person? Gus Morgan. From
day one.

However, as a new mother I was a wreck. Hormones are fuck-
ery. My parents stayed in LA long enough to celebrate Gus's one-
week birthday, and then they had to return to North Carolina.
I quickly spiraled into the freshman mistake of not having a
routine. Gus fed at horrible hours and never slept, and I lived
in the rocking chair in his nursery, too tired and broken to get
out of my pajamas. Finally, I took his baby bathtub into our large
shower and tried to clean myself up. I wrapped him in a towel and
wrapped another around myself when he started wailing. So I sat
down on a bench and fed him, and then something started dripping on my leg. Bursting into tears, I scanned the ceiling trying
to figure out where the leak was coming from. Jeff was leaving in
a couple of days to start filming a movie in Louisiana, and I was

a raw nerve. I couldn't believe the house was falling apart on top of everything else.

Jeff walked in and stopped dead in his tracks. "What are you doing?"

Sitting on a bench in the middle of our bathroom, in near hysterics, with a towel around my waist and our newborn breastfeeding, he'd caught me frantically examining the ceiling for the leak.

"Water's dripping on me!" I wailed.

He came toward me. "Honey, look down."

Friends, my ceiling was not leaking. I was lactating, from my other breast, on my own leg. And too damn tired to figure it out.

"I'm getting you help," Jeff said. "You can't say no."

I was across the country from my mother. I didn't have a relative nearby. None of my girlfriends was around. I was totally alone. So we hired Claudia the Superhero (aka Baby Nanny). She changed Gus's diapers and helped with bath time, but really, she was taking care of me. She made sure I ate and slept, and she taught me how to be a mother and how to be sure of myself.

Jeffrey was home for only short bursts of time. When he was, I wanted everything to be pleasant and fun. I never raised any issues. I didn't talk about going back to work, or Gus's doctor appointments, or anything hard that was going on in our lives. Then, when he was away, I would text him and bring up all the issues. It was a frustrating cycle complicated by the fact that as new parents and a new couple, clearly we needed to address some things.

I felt like Jeff was scared to be alone with me. Sometimes I was afraid he just wasn't that into me. We'd known each other for only a year. Even when he wasn't working, he busied himself at home. Or he'd tell me, "Hey, I've got to take a meeting." I knew he didn't have a meeting. He just wanted to get on his motorcycle and go for a ride. He hadn't lived with a woman for a long time, and I'm a handful. That's not a mystery to me.

I realized I was putting a dumb amount of pressure on this man. He couldn't be my whole wide world. I had to make a life of my own. But here's the deal: I was the first of my friends to have a baby, and everyone else still wanted to have dinner in sexy, dimly lit places at 9 p.m. But by 6 p.m. each day I was catatonic. Trolling the neighborhood for other moms didn't help much either. I'd push Gus's stroller around the neighborhood and occasionally see other people, but they'd have ear buds in and sunglasses on and a stony look on their faces. It wasn't like in North Carolina where everyone says hello to each other.

So when Gus was three months old I booked a job on *White Collar* and rented a two-bedroom, furnished apartment in New York City from people who would be in Martha's Vineyard for the summer. Jeff was going to come be with us once he wrapped the movie he was shooting, and his parents planned to visit at the end of June.

When I showed up in New York, I discovered that the apartment was blanketed in cat fur and the family's stuff was piled up all over the place. Since Jeffrey is massively allergic to cats, I knew I had to remedy the situation, and I had to do it in a couple of days with an infant. I bought a vacuum cleaner and went to town, but the fur had colonized the furniture, so I bought fabric to cover the couches and chairs just to have a place where I could put Gus down.

On top of everything, the apartment was sweltering. When Jeff arrived, I was in poor shape. It was the day before my birthday, and Jeff popped his head into the bedroom and announced, "Hil, I'm going to go run an errand."

"What?"

My eyes must have turned into carving knives because he quickly said, "I have to go find you a present."

Maybe I should have been grateful, but I didn't want him to leave. I felt like I hadn't seen him since Gus's birth. The movie he had just wrapped up had been about a horrific subject, so he was acting withdrawn and sad. Even when we were together, I had no idea how to reach him. I didn't want some *thing*, I just wanted him to *be* with us. I wanted him to have missed me while we were apart and to have daydreamed about what we'd do when we were finally back in the city together. It was exactly one year since that faint pink pregnancy test line had showed up in our lives. I wanted to feel like our relationship had grown deeper.

"I don't want a present," I told him. "Let's just do something together." But off he went.

Jeff's parents were visiting, and so I spent the day with them. They knew I was disappointed, although I tried to be upbeat. Hours later, Jeff returned. I pretended everything was fine.

The next morning his parents were flying back home and we were under a time crunch, so I had to open presents immediately. In my family, birthdays are a whole-day-long affair, and presents are the very last thing you get into. The grand finale, if you will. Here I was, barely into my first cup of coffee, and it was go go go. Grinning, Jeff handed me a box, wrapped by someone else in creamy white paper.

Inside was a small, black box. When I snapped back the top, I saw a white gold watch with diamonds glittering all over the band. A mother of pearl face mooned at me. It was very feminine and pretty, but it wasn't me. Not even a little.

The room felt small. The air conditioning was insufficient against the swampy summer day. I wanted to go for a walk by myself. I wanted to weep. I wanted to scream. I'd had a baby with a stranger who didn't know me at all.

I choked out a thank you.

Jeffrey's parents left to catch their plane, and instead of talking to Jeffrey about it, I spent the day stewing, hormones a-raging. *This motherfucker doesn't know anything about me. He's just buying me a shiny thing to try to distract me because he doesn't like who I really am.*

I was crushed that he couldn't find something that had meaning, like the gift he'd given me in New Mexico. I come from a family of makers. We craft each other long-thought-out gifts. My dad makes hand-planed cutting boards from wood he's chopped himself. My mother makes beautiful scrapbooks of our childhood for us kids to take into adulthood. My brother John wrote Gus a book of fairy tales, complete with a handmade shield and sword. Conrad does photography projects. Billy made me paintings.

Jeff asked me what was wrong, and I snapped, "You bought me a watch Jeffrey. I don't even wear a watch."

Hurt, he replied, "I just wanted you to have a nice thing." *He wanted me to have a nice thing. That's all.* I cringe now thinking of how hard I'd been on him for something so stupid. But in the moment I couldn't apologize or say thank you and mean it. I wanted him to understand that I didn't want shiny jewelry and expensive things. I didn't want us to be superficial or material. There was a part of him that he hadn't fully explored yet, and that is what I wanted. I'd caught a glimpse of it when we'd first gotten together, driving around looking for buffalo in the desert. The rancher. The dreamer. The man who put Christmas lights on everything. But I didn't say any of that.

He stormed out of the house, went for a walk with the dogs, and didn't come back until four in the morning.

A week later he left to start another movie in Kerhonkson, New York.

I was working on *White Collar* and Jeff was two and a half hours from the city, but he might as well have been across the country. We weren't on the same page at all. Our communication had dwindled to simple text exchanges.

> Me: Did you get to the cabin OK?
> Jeffrey: Yes. No traffic.
> Me: OK, good. Talk to you later.

The future became a haze, impossible to visualize. We didn't have a place that felt like home. We hadn't planned past the getting pregnant phase. Under that big New Mexico sky, our life had been beautifully mapped out. It all seemed so tangible and absolute. The heartbreak of realizing that maybe we'd been wrong and there wouldn't be a ranch or a shop or a Christmas tree farm was creeping in. We had no idea how we were going to do any of that while Jeff had to work. The fantasy had worn thin.

To make matters worse, he was having a hell of a time on the movie learning to play guitar and sing. A perfectionist, he got incredibly frustrated that it wasn't coming easily. And he had to do it in front of an entire festival of people. He was really intimidated by it, and some of that angst got displaced on me.

One night on the phone he barked, "Well, if you guys were here, I wouldn't be so stressed out."

I'd like to tell you I hopped in a car and rushed to his side without a thought, but that would be a lie. I called my manager, Meg, to unload, but she wasn't having it. "Hilarie, you are a grownup sweetie. You are a mother. I know you know how to rent a car. Rent a car and go out there."

Meg Mortimer has flaming red hair, talks very fast, and is *all* New York. She partied at Studio 54. She's been married a couple of times. She loves theater and art and fun. The embodiment of fabulous, she has lived in a way that gives her an expertise in life and love. "But, but, but," I protested.

"Hilarie, do you want to be right? Or do you want to be happy? Go."

I packed up the baby swing, dismantled the crib, rented a car, printed out directions, put four-month-old Gus in his car seat, and listened to him scream for two hours while I asked myself over and over, "What am I doing?"

I arrived at a tiny A-frame cabin Jeff had rented that was nestled in a lush stand of red oaks and sycamores. We were in the middle of nowhere, with no neighbors to be seen anywhere.

Jeff raced out into the driveway to greet us. The awkwardness that had plagued us during those back-and-forth months melted away. He was softer out there in the chirpy, dim woods. The cabin was rustic and spare, decidedly different from the hot, cluttered city apartment. There weren't any bedrooms, but there was a small loft. It was so quiet and smelled like where I grew up, like grass and tomatoes and dirt.

Twilight was blanketing the sky, and Jeff led us out into the backyard. The dogs had been miserable in the city, cooped up and leashed. But here, Bisou and our new puppy, Bandit, rolled in deer dung, darted into the woods, chased squirrels, and gleefully ran free.

I picked a bunch of wildflowers and put them in a glass Coca-Cola bottle Jeff had left on the counter. As I set the flowers on the table, Jeff noticed and nodded. "That's better," he said. That tiny moment—his seeing me trying to make things beautiful and valuing it—imprinted on my heart.

I woke up early, encouraged by the easy sunrise, and made Jeff a pot of coffee.

"You guys wanna come to set today?" He wanted us there.

I spent lazy days plopping Gus in his baby carrier and going on long walks. I'd pick Queen Anne's lace, discover little roads and hidden cabins, and visit a farmers' market with meat and vegetables from the neighboring farms.

On one of Jeff's days off I asked him whether he wanted to join me and Gus. He did. It was the closest thing we'd had to a date in ages.

Down the road sat a fabulous white cabin. We'd never seen anything like it before—part modern, part rustic. It was art.

"Let's get a little closer," he whispered.

With two dogs and a baby, Jeff and I were not so stealthily creeping down the driveway when two men came out the front door. I was nervous. We were definitely trespassing, and someone walking out of a house with a shotgun wouldn't be at all odd around there.

"Hello," they called out. No guns drawn.

Jeff hollered back, "Oh. Sorry. Your house is beautiful. We were just admiring it."

"Come on inside." Just like that, they opened their home to us. In my brain I ran through all the *Dateline* episodes I'd devoured in my lifetime and weighed the risk of following strangers. If they were killers, they were chic as hell. Jeff and I looked at each other and then said, "Okay."

One of the men was an artist from Central America, and the house had fabulous bursts of color and paintings from the floor up to the huge vaulted ceilings.

We told the couple all about our time in New Mexico and having Gus. They told us all about their lives and then fed us, total strangers who'd invaded their home, heaping bowls of paella, which they had just made.

As we left, hours later, with a huge Tupperware container of leftovers, they said, "You guys are going to love it here."

The fantasy was back.

As I packed to go back to the city, Jeff called out, "Real quick, before you go, I found this cabin online last night. It's in Rhinebeck. You wanna go see it?" I didn't really think it would come to anything, but we were back in the land of possibility.

"Sure babe."

"Oh good. I already called the agent." Somebody was excited.

Coffee

When I was a kid, drinking coffee was the most adult, cool, sophisticated thing you could do. My parents drank it all day long, and still do. During the holidays, when we're all together, it isn't unheard-of for them to make a fresh pot at 9 p.m.

The second I moved out of the house when I turned eighteen, I splurged what little money I had on good coffee from fancy gourmet shops in New York City. We worked such odd hours on *One Tree Hill* that my parents' twenty-four-hour coffee habit took hold of me as though part of my DNA. It became my routine, my moment of solace. Making coffee exactly to one's own taste is an incredibly personal ritual.

It can also be a powerful way to say "I love you." Noticing how someone takes their coffee and making it just right is as foxy as it gets. Before I'd met Jeffrey, my hairdresser, Jojo—a southern powerhouse of a woman—taught me some love magic. "Sprinkle some cinnamon in the grounds before you brew the coffee. Gives it warmth. It'll make a man cuckoo in love with you."

She was not wrong.

I loved getting up before sunrise and making Jeffrey coffee before work each morning, never letting on that I'd cast a love spell on his caffeine.

Now, with life at the farm, making the coffee is the one moment of calm before the day snowballs. I wake up before the kids, start the pot, deliver a cup to Jeffrey's nightstand, and then feed George and Gus while nursing that first glorious cup. It's when I make my lists and cuddle my kids, mentally preparing for whatever life is going to throw at us that day.

* * *

In a world where chaos abounds, making coffee is ceremonial and an act of self-care. Here are a few tips:

* If you wanna get real fancy, I highly suggest taking the time to use a French press. The coffee comes out richer and fuller bodied.

* If you suffer from allergies, try replacing sugar with local honey.

* What to do with all those coffee grounds? Put them in your garden. Not only do they repel pests like slugs, fruit flies, and mosquitos, they add nitrogen and improve drainage, aeration, and water retention in the soil. Coffee grounds are especially good for blueberries and azaleas, and you can use them to help keep your hydrangeas blue.

* Mix them with some coconut oil to make a body scrub that fights cellulite.

* And if you're like Jeffrey, a little after-dinner nightcap of coffee and Baileys Irish Cream is the best way to settle in after a long day of chopping wood and generally being macho.

The truth was, I'd been searching since childhood for a place where I felt I fit in. I was that weird, loud kid with huge glasses, big frizzy hair, and teeth coming out in every direction. Beginning in third grade I insisted on wearing nothing but black every day, so I'm sure it isn't surprising that I was the odd duck. That was the year I started doing theater at the local high school. Onstage, it didn't matter that I was a strange little girl; I was a part of something beautiful and moving and fun. All I wanted was to be an actor and to get the hell out of Virginia. I wanted it so bad, in fact, that my entire senior year I talked with a fake New York accent. *If you build it, it will come.* And it did. I got a scholarship to Fordham College at Lincoln Center and began my new life as a big city lady. I never would have admitted it then, but now I can look back and see how much I longed for wide open spaces. In the city, I planted random bulbs in trays on my window sills, hungry for the green of my childhood.

Then I got offered a role in a pilot called *Ravens* about a small-town basketball team. The show was narrated by the wise old coach as he explained the goings-on of the town to his dead wife. It was folksy and sweet and filmed in a town where my family had vacationed when I was a kid. Wilmington, North Carolina, felt a little bit like I was going home. After a few years of feeling boxed in, in New York City, I was happy to find the kind of town I'd grown up in, full of parades and tradition and community.

But as *Ravens* became *One Tree Hill*, it was rebranded as a sexy show about teenagers with adult problems. I was in over my head, but it afforded me the ability to buy my first home, a Victorian built in 1880 with a tidy little front yard where I could plant a garden.

As you know by now, the Paris dream of wandering along the

Seine and taking in Versailles was not to be. And LA ate me up and spit me out. If Jeffrey was willing to try this new place in Rhinebeck on for size, why the hell not? At that point, I'd give any town a whirl. Perhaps it could be the place where I fit, the place I longed to find.

That day, driving into Rhinebeck, we both could tell something was happening.

After our stop at the candy store, we loaded back into the rented SUV and meandered out of town on the hunt for Jeff's dream cabin. To get there, you cruise along the 9G, passing a postmodern Stonehenge—wonderful sculptures composed of huge boulders and stray car parts. Sheep grazed high atop a hill on the left. We turned onto West Pine Road, a shady street dotted with little ramblers and split-level homes like the ones I grew up in. The street dead-ended into a little cul-de-sac, backed by a stand of trees. I thought we'd taken a wrong turn until Jeff announced, "This is it," as he eased the car onto a long gravel driveway bordered by tall wild grass and some big apple trees.

It was quiet, and no one else was around. I was struck by the thought, *He wants to be all alone with me.* Jeff liked who I was at the Kerhonkson cabin, and I liked who I was there too.

We rounded a curve in the driveway, and there was a Davy Crockett cabin. The frontiersman is something of a Burton family mascot. My dad is a Davy Crockett nut, so my brothers and I were Davy Crockett nuts. My mother used to rock me to sleep singing, "Born on a mountaintop in Tennessee . . ." An autographed picture of Fess Parker hanging over our kitchen table was the pride and joy of our family. My dad never believed in marking up one's body, but in his sixties he eased up, and my brother Billy and I went with him to get his first tattoo. We all got Davy Crockett artwork. Old Betsy, Crockett's long rifle, runs the length of my ribs, pointed forward to ward off predators. It peeked out from behind the dress I was wearing the night I met Jeffrey. "Let me see what you got there," he said, leaning in to examine the firearm as we stood in his living room. Then, without warning, he very lightly kissed it. Now, here we were standing in front of a Davy Crockett cabin. We didn't even need to go inside.

The realtor wasn't there yet, so we hiked around the twelve wooded acres that surrounded the cabin. There's a pretty steep hill in those woods that leads down to a reservoir. I scrambled down it, with Gus strapped to my chest and Jeff holding my hand, the three of us swaying from sapling to sapling. There were big outcroppings of stone, little clearings where I imagined us building a teepee, and Jeff was excited about cutting trails to ride around on with an ATV. The dogs ran with abandon.

Gus was alert and curious, wanting to grab all the leaves. He loved the way his feet felt on different things—a plush pile of moss or the rough grooves of tree bark. We discovered a fuzzy caterpillar and then headed back up to the house.

The real estate agent still wasn't there, so we settled into the porch swing. The air smelled of wood and water. I took a deep breath and said, "Okay. Let's do it."

"Really?" Jeff grinned and then asked me again, "Really? You're not freaked out by this?"

I laughed and shook my head no. "I can do all this. I was born to do this."

"Alright Laura Ingalls," Jeff teased.

The real estate agent, Rick Reilly, was a sweet guy with a soft spot for kids. After he showed up, we walked through the house with him, and I could see that the kitchen was a project. It was a dark six-by-six-foot square with 1970s heavily trimmed cabinetry and orange Formica countertops. In my brain I was already making Home Depot lists. But there was a big upstairs loft bedroom and a nursery off of that. Downstairs were two more bedrooms begging for more kids. One bathroom was a 1950s baby blue, and the other had a marigold bathtub and sink. It was going to be a lot of work.

Jeff announced, "We'll offer them the asking price. Let's close really quick."

The next day, before the deal was even done, we snuck back onto the property. Jeff wanted to look at the outbuildings—a huge two-story barn and a couple of old sheds—places to tinker. While he was poking around, I noticed something glimmering under the porch. It was the house key.

I dangled it out for Jeff to see and whispered, "Wanna break in?" As if anyone would have heard me. Then we furtively let ourselves in to our new home.

3

I went looking for my dreams outside of
myself and discovered, it's not what the world
holds for you, it's what you bring to it.

—attributed to L. M. Montgomery

We wanted to have Thanksgiving at the cabin, but it needed so much work. I had tackled plenty of renovations on my home in Wilmington, but I had no idea about septic fields or propane gas or heating systems. Plus this time, I had a deadline, an infant, and was still working on *White Collar* while Jeff was working down in New Orleans.

In mid-November I flew into JFK with Gus on a Monday, rented a minivan, and thanked my lucky stars that my little brother John was coming to help. John had been in China for three years and was coming home for his first break since leaving. He'd never met Gus. Hell, he'd never even met Jeffrey. My brother and I did, however, have a family history of doing home renovation projects together.

When I was growing up, our first family project was stripping wallpaper in the house on Ithaca Road in Sterling Park. The family room wallpaper was horrible, tan with intricate brown drawings that looked like old advertisements from a turn-of-the-century newspaper. In the kitchen the wallpaper was printed with oppressively enormous grapes, oranges, and apples. My brothers and I had a ball trying to see who could pull the longest strips down.

Since then, we have whitewashed fences and built furniture and removed popcorn ceiling in various Burton properties. Conrad is the patient one. Billy is the organized one. And John is an ox. His help on the cabin was perfectly timed.

John landed at 6 a.m. Tuesday after a long overnight flight, took a train to meet me in midtown Manhattan, and we hit the ground running. Since there was no furniture at the cabin yet, we rented rooms across the Hudson River at an extended-stay chain hotel. Each morning, we'd run over to my beloved Home Depot, collect whatever materials we needed for the cabin's transformation that day, and then with baby in tow, we'd drive across the river and down the shady road to our new little sanctuary.

Gus, thank God, was the easiest baby on the planet. I'd put him down on the one section of carpeted flooring in the dining room, and he'd play with Thomas the Train for hours. Or he'd coo in his swing, rocking back and forth while watching John and me dart all over the house. The previous homeowners had been meticulous in taking care of their home, and so our task was to merely brighten up the joint and bring it up to the twenty-first century.

We started in the main living space and spider-webbed out. We took off cabinet doors and sanded and primed every inch of that dark oppressive wood. John set up a door-painting station down in the basement so Gus wouldn't crawl all over them. I'd always wanted to try one of those Rust-Oleum countertop refinishing kits. Who can resist that Cinderella transformation of turning pumpkin-orange Formica into a subtle, relaxing neutral? (I can hear all the hipsters out there lamenting that I didn't preserve the garish original fixtures—*How could you?* My friends, it was easy!)

While cabinetry dried, we assembled a new crib and coordinated deliveries of a couch and new appliances. The propane guy gave me a newcomer lesson in fuel. We replaced sink fixtures and added new lighting to the intensely dark home.

Jeff has a thing about red bedrooms. For any of you *One Tree Hill* fans out there, you'll recall that my character Peyton Sawyer did too. Even her record label was called Red Bedroom Records. So a couple gallons of Ben Moore later, our loft bedroom had gone from bland to cozy and a bit mysterious.

Since the house was so tiny, storage was massively important. There were virtually no closets, and so I commissioned a local furniture maker to create a one-of-a-kind bed with drawers underneath as a surprise for Jeffrey. As Thanksgiving approached, everyone was winding down, and I begged and begged them to deliver before the break. My experience living in Los Angeles had prepped me to get blown off, but instead, the furniture maker promised me he'd be there on Friday. That was perfect! Jeff was wrapping his movie in Louisiana and would be driving up to our new home on Sunday.

TVs were installed, curtains were hung, a storage container was delivered from North Carolina. My dad kindly packed up furniture from my Wilmington Victorian and things from his antique store and sent them up. Gus tumbled around in the empty boxes as we organized. Sheets. Dishes. Bookcases. The dining table and chairs.

By the time we finished up for the day on Thursday, we were exhausted. John and I had lived on a steady diet of Gatorade, granola bars, and Wendy's. We treated ourselves that night to dinner at the Friendly's next to the hotel. It was such a throwback to our childhood, getting hotdogs after Little League baseball games, that we couldn't resist. I was happy working side by side with my brother again, plotting and planning and making shit happen. Eating our hot dogs that night, we were a bit smug. We had two and a half more days before Jeff showed up. We could afford to ease up a bit.

Friday morning, we took our time checking out of the hotel. We did one more Home Depot and Target run and then made our way to the cabin. The bed was due to arrive in the afternoon, so we unpacked and made lists of what still needed to be done.

My phone dinged with a text from Jeff.

> **Jeff:** How's it going?
> **Me:** Super good. Can't wait for you to get here.
> **Jeff:** See you in 4 hours!

Wait, what?

> **Me:** I thought you were still working. Didn't think you were coming till Sunday!
> **Jeff:** Got off early! Been driving all night. Love you!

Shit! "JOHN," I hollered. "We gotta move!" Unpacked boxes full of odds and ends were stacked all over the place. The cabinet doors still lay drying in the basement. Tile for the kitchen backsplash was still in its packaging.

You know those design shows that are massively overproduced, where homeowners have to renovate within a certain amount of time? I don't wanna brag, but John and I would be good at that. We put our heads down and turned that cabin into the cutest fucking thing you ever saw. We kicked out rugs. Tossed throw pillows. Hung pictures. Placed books. Filled the storage container with empty boxes and packaging materials and slammed the door shut—*If you can't see it, it doesn't exist!*

At 3 p.m., the bed arrived! I tipped heavily and thanked the furniture maker profusely as I ushered him and his helpers out the door. We had one hour left. Gus still rocked in his swing, completely entertained by the chaos.

I threw up the tile on the backsplash while John reattached cabinet doors. We tossed the one Phillips head screwdriver we had back and forth as we attached hardware on the doors. The sound of gravel crunching in the driveway stopped us. "He's here!"

John focused on the last three drawer handles, while I lit a scented candle, put sweet Gus on my hip, and breathlessly opened the front door. "Honey! So glad you're here!"

Guys, I was *beat*. John was a zombie. But the look on Jeff's face when he saw his dream cabin all put together was something I'll always cherish. He walked from room to room, touching furniture and the new fridge and the curtains. "I love it," he said earnestly. "I just love it."

I was relieved. And Jeff's appreciation to John was the beginning of a strong friendship. He continued to take in the new space. "Not sure what you were in such a tizzy about. There was hardly anything to do. Place looks great."

John and I exchanged looks. We knew better.

Only one thing was left undone: we needed a new stove. The old stove was terrifying, to put it politely—and you can't have Thanksgiving without a fully functioning stove. Jeff is a nutcase about Thanksgiving. He does all the cooking. He had been fantasizing about our first cabin holiday since the day we visited the property. But he couldn't make his dream dinner on that stove. Multiple burners were inoperable. It made a scary clicking noise. And it was gas, making me fear the whole house would blow up if we used it.

I had ordered a stove that was scheduled to arrive days ahead of Thanksgiving. But then I got a call: "Orders are backed up because drivers are off for the holiday." Two days before Thanksgiving, still no stove. I harangued the delivery company. I jumped every time I imagined I heard tires on the gravel driveway. John and I had been cooking everything in a shitty toaster oven, and I'd lie awake at night trying to figure out how I could possibly make Thanksgiving dinner in it.

The day before Thanksgiving I heard the truck rumbling down the driveway, and I started screaming, "The stove is here!" The three of us adults ran out like kids on Christmas morning. It was the end of the day, and ours was the last delivery. The two delivery guys maneuvered the stove into the kitchen and went to connect the unit to the propane tank. "Ma'am, you're missing a piece."

"Huh?"

"There's a little safety valve. Connects the fuel source. Your old stove doesn't have it. Pretty dangerous. We can't connect the stove without it." Jeff started asking a million questions. "What do you mean? Can't you just hook it up anyway and we'll risk it? Where can we get it?" The guys were shaking their heads. It was like they didn't understand that the happiness of my entire family was resting upon this stove. Jeff already had a huge local turkey brining in the fridge.

"Best we can do is come back on Monday or Tuesday with the right part," they said. I was frantically googling appliance supply stores in the Hudson Valley and jumped on the phone.

"You have the valve?" A mom-and-pop shop across the river in Saugerties had exactly what we were looking for. But they were closing in twenty minutes.

"Please! Please stay open for me! I'll be there in nineteen minutes. Without it we won't be able to have Thanksgiving," I begged. There was a long pause.

"Okay. I'll be here."

I fixed my gaze on the delivery guys and said, "Look, please stay here. I'll give you any amount of money to just stay here."

"It's fine. We'll stick around. Go get that part."

I couldn't believe it. The store stayed open for me. The stove guys waited for me. Crossing the river in the dark, I was filled with gratitude. Just by asking people to be nice, they were nice. I wasn't in LA anymore. I could feel myself settling in.

Jeffrey made coffee for the delivery crew and entertained them while I shuttled back and forth across the river, so incredibly in love with our new community.

The next day, Jeff rose early and got to work in the kitchen. We all took turns in the baby-size kitchen, chopping and prepping, doing dishes, setting the table. John and Gus wore matching cable knit sweaters and wrestled. I focused on the pies.

The sun set and we lay out all the food across the dining table. John had missed eating the typical American fare while in China, and Jeff hadn't had a real meal the entire time he had been filming. There's something about constantly moving in high gear—when you have the opportunity to stop, you almost don't know how. But sitting down and saying grace for Thanksgiving, I took the moment in with great consciousness.

*Dear God. Thank you for our family. Thank
you for this new adventure. Thank you for this
happiness. Please help us to pay it forward.*

After Thanksgiving, John left, and Jeff, Gus, and I holed up in our cabin. Our biggest outings were to the candy store in Rhinebeck. Jeff learned that the elegant, curly-haired owner was Ira Gutner, and the store, Samuel's, was named after his late uncle Samuel. Ira and Uncle Samuel had an affinity for going to Yankee games, and before every game they'd stop at a penny candy store right outside of the stadium. In those aisles of sugary delight, Ira's uncle used candy to teach Ira everything he needed to know about the world of business. Ira grew up to become a successful entrepreneur in the fabric industry in Manhattan. He attributed all his success to those childhood lessons, and when he retired early and moved upstate, he opened up his own sweet shop and named it Samuel's.

Samuel's became a town headquarters for Jeff. He went there almost every day, under the guise of picking up something for me. Ira sold chocolate bark with sea salt and almonds and cranberries, and Jeff and I devoured it at an embarrassing speed. But Jeff also went there just to get coffee and talk to Ira—find out the gossip in town and what places to go and restaurants to try—and then he'd come home and share that information with me.

"There's a salvage place in Red Hook. That young guy who works at the shop? His parents run it. Might try to pop in." Or "Ira says we've got to try the French place in town—Le Petit Bistro. It ain't Paris, but it's supposed to be great." Or "Ira's gal that makes chocolate has a baby the same age as Gus and she wants to have a play date." Oh, Ira—dressed in his plaid shirts or turtleneck sweaters or overalls when he was feeling particularly "country." He was so invested in our happiness.

One of his first edicts was that we had to attend the Sinterklaas festival. A Christmas festival! I didn't need to be persuaded.

The Dutch brought the legend of Santa Claus to America in the 1600s when they settled here. In the mid-1980s, celebration-artist Jeanne Fleming brought the Dutch tradition back to life with a children's parade through the streets of Rhinebeck. Twenty years later, after much success as the director of the Greenwich Village Halloween parade, Jeanne came back in 2008 with a bevy of artists and musicians and resurrected the festival with the help of an army of townspeople. Sinterklaas, based on St. Nicholas, rides through the main drag in Kingston, on the other side of the river, and then crosses the Hudson on a boat covered with Christmas lights. He arrives at the train station where the Rhinebeck children greet him, hooting and laughing loudly. Then they parade through town.

Ira invited us to be his guests, which meant we had use of the bench outside the sweet shop. A good thing too, because not five minutes after we parked on one of the side streets and made our way over to Market Street, the whole town had congregated. Everybody was holding glowing white star lanterns with Christmas lights glimmering through the holes. A pack of children carrying

Turkey Wars

The very first Thanksgiving Jeffrey and I had together, he came to North Carolina to celebrate the holiday with my family. They'd met only once before. I was mildly nervous. "I'll make the turkey," my mother said. She'd made the turkey my whole life.

"No, no," Jeffrey replied. "*I'll* be making the turkey."

Good lord. It was like watching two alpha animals circle and size each other up before mauling one another. It was settled that they *both* would be making a turkey, and all our guests would vote on which was better. So Jeffrey and my mother went to town. Mom brined hers. Jeffrey went with injections for his. They jockeyed over oven space, and a copious amount of shit was talked.

But no one had considered what all the guests would be doing while this cook-off took place. Decades before, my preschool teacher Mrs. Allison had given my mother a recipe for "Witches Brew," a hot harvest drink meant to warm up even the coldest of days. As kids, we were given the booze-free version of this sugary treat (Mrs. Allison was fond of adding a splash of whiskey to her brew), but as grownups, we discovered that it lived up to its name as an instigator of debauchery. Naturally, this particular Thanksgiving during the Turkey Wars, Witches Brew was readily available and a huge hit with our crowd.

Before the first course even started, the adults had dissolved into a mess of giggles and unruliness. My friend Nick had wanted to contribute, and so he labored for days over a butternut squash bisque. Everyone cackled as he tried to steady himself enough to ladle it out at each place setting. By the time the turkeys were presented for judgment, it was a lost cause. Jeff tried my mother's. "It's fabulous," he admitted. My mother sampled his recipe. "Oh God, that's good!" she exclaimed.

What had started off as a wildly stressful cage match became a love-fest of food, family, and friends. And I had the Witches Brew to thank.

Witches Brew

Keep in mind that this recipe is from the 1980s!

6 tea bags of your choice (I use a spice tea)
1 can frozen orange juice
1 can frozen lemonade
3 cinnamon sticks
1 tablespoon cloves

Grab the biggest pot in your kitchen and add 4 quarts of water. Bring to a slow boil and add the tea bags. Let steep for 7 minutes. Remove the tea bags and add the frozen juice, lemonade, cinnamon sticks, and cloves. Simmer on medium heat for at least 30 minutes. To serve, strain out the spices and ladle into a teacup. Splash in a healthy dose of whiskey to make it interesting.

pine branches festooned with tinsel led the parade. The most beautiful Sinterklaas/Santa Claus followed with a long, snowy beard and bright robes of crushed red velvet. Then a wild puppet show swirled down the street. The puppets, which are two stories tall, careened along while all of us cheered and clapped.

Gus nestled up on Jeff's shoulders, and we huddled together, limbs numb, chins and noses frozen and red. We had become dots in a sea of Christmas cheer—a part of something. The drums of the marching bands kept the entire town in rhythm, everyone dancing together to create warmth. Costumed marchers tossed candy to the kids perched on the curbs for a closer look. Alpacas and donkeys in elaborate South American harnesses pranced down the main drag like royalty.

We took Gus to his first Christmas Eve service at a handsome little chapel down the road. The elderly congregation oohed and aahed over our funny little boy, who clapped and sang "ba ba ba ba" during the hymns. Christmas Day was a tiny, intimate affair—just Jeffrey, Gus, and me. We taught him how to open presents for the first time, burning the wrapping in the roaring fire Jeff built.

In his red long underwear, purchased proudly from the Rhine-beck Department Store, Jeff opened his gift from me. A note in the box said "Go to the garage." With the help of my dad, we'd gotten the local ATV dealer to stealthily deliver a Yamaha Rhino so Jeff could tear around the woods. Figuring that eventually we'd need to plow the incredibly long driveway, it was also a functional tool, as well as a ridiculously fun one. Jeff was like a little kid. Our quiet cul-de-sac was now filled with the roaring of the Rhino's engine and Jeff's whooping. "Be careful!" I called out.

He skidded to a stop. "You and Gus get dressed and get in here!"

Together we played all day like children. And the next day, as if on cue, it snowed twenty-four inches.

In February, Jeff was off to Canada to do a project and then stuck in LA doing press for a bit. I was working on *White Collar* when spring arrived. Sometimes on my day off I'd get a babysitter to stay in the city with Gus so I could drive to the cabin and mow the lawn or paint the shed for a few hours. Being up there and doing something with my hands calmed me. I felt entirely alone and peaceful. In Rhinebeck I was comfortable in my own skin. I could go to the hardware store with no makeup and wearing my dad's old fatigues. And unlike in LA, I had people to say hello to.

Our neighbor, Farmer Mike, was a former firefighter and a great storyteller. He had lived right there in that tiny community forever, raising kids who had long since left the nest. He knew every person who lived on the street and knew who lived in their houses before they did. Mike's wife, Marcia, made lovely paintings of all the lighthouses in the Hudson Valley. She invited us to tour her studio and gifted us with a painting that we hung in the cabin.

Mike hung NO TRESPASSING signs for us, and when we weren't around, he chased off kids who snuck onto our property to ride their dirt bikes. He reminded me of my dad, always prepared for worst-case scenarios. Mike told us where to buy a huge shipping container to store supplies and how to live off the land. Once, our clothes dryer went haywire and started smoking. It wasn't on fire, but we weren't sure what to do, so we called the volunteer fire department and told them it wasn't an emergency but it would be great if they could send someone out. Mike, who used to hang around listening to the scanner, arrived before the first fire truck showed up. Gus and I avoided the fray and sat in the car down the driveway. It must have been a slow day, because no fewer than five trucks showed up, from all different parts of the county. Mike was gladly on hand to greet and communicate with each one.

We learned from Mike that an entire family lived right along our road. Bob and his wife, Rachel, are lovely people about my age. Her parents lived two doors down from us, her older sister lived a few doors down from them, and her aunt and uncle lived just three houses down from them. Rachel grew up playing with the kids who lived in our house and knew our property better than I did. They had heard that I collected taxidermy, and when they came by to introduce themselves, Bob showed up with a fox pelt. The fox had been killed by a car, and as a taxidermist Bob recognized that it was too beautiful to just leave on the road, so he'd tended the hide and brought it to us as a welcome-to-the-neighborhood gift. I thought, *These are my people.*

Williams Lumber is a dynasty in the Hudson Valley, run by the patriarch, Stacy, and his children. That first year, Jeffrey and I were in the Rhinebeck location just about every day. We became familiar with the staff, and I'm pretty sure they laughed whenever we left.

"You all need anything else?" they'd ask as we checked out.

"I'm sure we'll think of something," we'd respond.

They knew everything about what we were working on—whether it was painting the hallway or tiling the bathroom. I quickly learned that in a small town, everybody knows your business. It becomes a town affair, and you just have to get comfortable with that. The anonymity of our days in LA and NYC was gone. Quickly, we felt like we were part of something.

The whole front yard was filled with brambles of wild roses. It was a gorgeous stronghold of thorns, ready to make a pincushion out of Gus, so Jeffrey and I pulled them all out. We cleared the area around the house of the brambles and saplings, and then we started experimenting with what would grow in our shady yard. The soil was totally different from the soil in North Carolina and California. We planted a couple of Christmas trees in the front yard because we knew that was the end game. Once we had our first spring and saw the apple and peach orchards, Jeff got excited about all the flowering trees. He missed his bougainvillea back in LA, so he went to the nursery and picked out one of every flowering tree that they had. "We'll just plant them all and see what happens," he said.

I got window boxes and painted them red to pop against the dark logs of the cabin. I mixed taller annuals like aster with more compact blooms, always adding a bit of creeping Jenny. That had been my secret-weapon plant down in North Carolina; it grew anywhere and came back year after year. But I learned they don't call it that up north.

"Can you tell me where to find the creeping Jenny?" I inquired. It was as though I'd asked for the local peeping Tom. The raised eyebrows and tilted heads hinted that I'd made a mistake. "It's like a vine, tiny roundish leaves . . . kind of neon green?"

"Oh, you mean the aurea?" Sure. Aurea. That's what we'll call it now.

The only open, sunlit space at the cabin was on top of the septic system. And I really didn't want to grow food in a septic field. Instead, I planted forsythia, impatiens, and woodland flowers that grow well in rocky soil. Jeff and I actually got into a fight about the forsythia. As a West Coast boy, he had never seen it, and the neon yellow of the blossoms captivated him. Huge hedges of the flowering bushes lined the roads and sent up fireworks of flowers in front of the businesses in town. But I was dead set against them. My entire life my father had told us stories about his mother sending him to the forsythia bushes to pick out the switch she would whip him with. He hated them. Which meant I hated them. All Burtons hated them. Jeffrey brought five of them home anyway. Ugh, the betrayal. I had to admit though, they were striking.

I was becoming less Burton, more Morgan.

To help balance the two, I planted tulips and irises and all the bulbs that my mom and her Dutch family grew. Her bulbs were a sight to behold when I was growing up: crocuses, then daffodils, then tulips, and then the lilies of summer. It was a parade of grandeur.

Ira also sent us over to Hoffman's Barn, a nondescript treasure trove hidden in the back of a movie theater parking lot. Roger and Pam Hoffman found the beauty in the bygone: an entire building full of old doors and windows; another building segmented into sections dedicated to china, bureaus, wingback chairs, hatchets, and kids' toys; outside, rusted farm equipment, old logging saws, and various jewels in all shapes and forms. Roger came out and showed us around, and Pam, shy but warm, immediately made us feel at ease.

They both doted on Gus, explaining to him what the old tools and toys were. Gus was going through a massive John Henry phase.

Roger ushered him over to a low shelf of hammers—sledgehammers, rubber mallets, framing hammers. It was the island of lost toys for freaks like us who like tools that come with a narrative. Roger selected a huge wooden mallet with scars and tiny chunks missing. That mallet had seen action. "For you, John Henry," he said, handing the surprisingly light tool to Gus. There's not a toy in the world that could have compared with that gift.

Everything I've ever needed I've found at Hoffman's Barn. In the summer we bought some wooden half barrels and filled them with herbs. And when my birthday rolled around, Jeff went out to Hoffman's and found an old tractor seat that he mounted and placed in a wooden frame he built himself. He had made me some "fart"— that's "farm art." The stark contrast between my previous birthday and this one, made up of crafts and time spent together, was balm for my heart. We had grown together as a couple, as a family. This was who we were meant to be—as individuals and artists and as a couple.

We kept the house in LA, but the truth is that once we were in the cabin with its shitty kitchen, weird linoleum floor, Technicolor bathrooms, leaky windows, and creaky front door, we never wanted to leave. On paper, the LA house was a great family house, but we didn't feel like a family there. We felt like a family in the one-thousand-square-foot cabin.

4

She asked me whether I had learned to like big
cities. "I'd always be miserable in a city. I'd
die of lonesomeness. I like to be where I know
every stack and tree, and where all the ground
is friendly. I want to live and die here."

—Willa Cather, *My Antonia*

By the time December rolled around the following
year, we'd found a groove, but still we were all coming
and going in dizzying patterns. My youngest brother,
Conrad, was graduating from college, and I went home to North
Carolina for his graduation. John was finally home for good,
and it was the first time my whole family was going to be together in three years. Jeffrey wasn't working, but he decided not
to go with me. I was hot about it, but I didn't say anything out-
right; in fact, I barely said anything at all.

Jeff called me from Los Angeles. "I miss you guys so much. Are
you having fun?"

"We're having a great time. You're missing it." I said shortly.

The next night when we spoke, I reported, "We took Gus to see
Santa. You missed it." I was really disappointed, and my family was
a bit insulted. It was a sore spot.

We were doing Christmas in LA that year, and Jeff's way of making it up to me after not going to my brother's graduation was to agree to go to church on Christmas Eve. (He's convinced every year that he's going to burst into flames at church. It hasn't happened. Yet.) So the three of us set out to go to the children's service at a little nondenominational church in Studio City.

Outside the church was a living nativity. Donkeys, alpacas, sheep, and cows roamed around in the front yard of the church, with men and women in Jerusalem's finest fashions tending to them. Little kids dressed as angels shrieked with laughter as they ran through the crowds, goosing people with their wings. "This is adorable!" I yelled to Jeff over the chaos. He grinned as Gus, now a highly active toddler, plowed through the sea of bodies to get to the animals. Gus reached his hand out and screamed with giggles when a goat nibbled at him. Then the church bell rang.

Suddenly, nothing was adorable anymore. Whoever had the bright idea to put the fun stuff *before* the service did not take into account that kids are unreasonable creatures. No amount of "We can see 'em after the service, buddy!" could calm the storm that was Gus. Folks around us started up with the fan favorite "Joy to the World" as our boy flung himself into the aisle and ran to the big double doors and banged on them with balled fists.

Side note: Please don't think we are negligent parents. I'm a stickler for manners and good behavior. Our boy was widely known for tipping his hat to ladies (a trick Jeff had taught him) and acting like a little adult. But these barnyard creatures were his kryptonite!

Jeff looked at me. "Do you want to stay?"

"No," I said, crestfallen. I had just wanted to sing "The Little Drummer Boy" with Gus folded in my arms.

"Do you want to drive around and look at Christmas lights?" Jeff asked.

"Yeah, I guess so."

We drove in the dark and listened to carols on the radio. It was lovely, but it also felt very quiet and very small. Having come from celebrating with my big family, it felt hollow out in LA without our relatives or community. I'd gotten used to the bustle of our Hudson Valley life and constantly running into familiar faces. Trying to function in LA was harder than ever before.

The next morning Jeff made coffee and we opened gifts. Gus tore into his presents, and then I got up to go make breakfast, feeling the letdown of a holiday ending.

"Hold on, there's something in the tree," Jeff said.

I looked, and there was a white envelope that read "HILARIE." I opened it up, thinking it was a gift certificate. But inside was a piece of paper that read "MORGAN."

I turned around, and Jeffrey was down on one knee with the ring.

I wept. *He* wept. And then he explained that he'd stayed back in LA rather than go to North Carolina because he was in the process of designing and buying my ring. I felt like such an ass for giving him a hard time! (Big life lesson kids. Just don't be an ass. You never know when someone is planning a sweet surprise!) Meanwhile my entire family was very smug that the secret had been kept and I was finally gonna be a bonafide married lady.

"Do you guys have a date in mind yet?" my mom asked.

"We're working on it," I assured her. And we were. Jeff and I would zero in on a month, and then Jeff would book a job. We'd pick another date, and then I would book a gig.

I also wondered whether it was silly to get married when we were already living as husband and wife. I certainly didn't need a party. I wanted wedding planning to be enjoyable, and it wasn't. So we decided to back-burner the wedding. "We'll do it when it's super fun," I said, and kissed Jeffrey.

At the cabin I took a lot of pride in trying to fulfill the same duties that my mom had while I was growing up. I liked being self-sufficient. I liked being able to say that I was doing everything. I'd look at a magazine on Tuesday and decide I was going to build a window bench seat. I'd paint the walls the next day. Then I'd do the trim. Then I'd figure out the curtains. The cabin was an evolving renovation. Our visions for our life and our home were evolving too. We went on walks together in the woods and dreamed stuff up.

While I still worked down in NYC, my brother Billy came out from LA to help when Jeff had knee surgery. All this rugged living took a toll on my former high school basketball star. His knees had always been an issue, and we were assured that the surgeon in town, Andrew Stewart, was the very best. And he was. Billy helped Jeff out around the cabin and looked after Gus. And a couple of days after the surgery, the two of them decided to buy a huge wooden swing set to assemble in the yard, complete with a tower and a slide. So much for taking it easy.

Jeffrey has always played sentimental characters that sweep

women off their feet with gentle words and thoughtful inclusions. Real-life Jeff? Well, he's an entirely different kind of magic man. He pays compliments only when he really means them. He is 100 percent about actions over words. And so one spring morning, over coffee, Jeffrey asked, "Wanna build a fire pit today?" That's Jeff's code for: I'd like to spend time with you. Exactly my kind of romance.

There was a small portion of stone wall along the back of our property. It had fallen in on itself and wasn't doing much good keeping the deer or teenagers on dirt bikes out. So we salvaged the stones, heaving them into the back of the Rhino until we'd loaded the bed well past capacity. Once back at the site he'd prepped for the fire pit, we worked in tandem finding exactly the right stones to fit together. He could have taken me on a jet to Paris for dinner and it wouldn't have meant half as much as building that pit together. Once the steel ring was completely covered, Jeff gleefully leaped into Boy Scout mode, building his base of kindling and tinder to create a roaring blaze that burned through the wet springtime chill.

In the spring we started going to the Rhinebeck farmers' market every Sunday in the town's municipal parking lot. We'd walk from one white-tented booth to another, collecting a colorful riot of vegetables and fruits. The very frank cheesemonger dictated recommendations to each customer. "You're going to try this," I heard her announce to the older man in front of me. Then she fixed me with her stern gaze and handed me a piece of cheese. "You're going to like this one." I had blind faith in her ability to read my cheese fortune. There were the woodworkers who made cutting boards out of wood from the trees on their property, a beekeeper with a huge

The Want-To Creates the How-To

Things I've built: A bar. A couch. A King-size bed. Multiple coffee tables. A bathroom vanity. Outdoor furniture. Bookshelves. Raised garden beds. And it all started with a fireplace mantel at my parents' house.

The house I was born in had a huge handmade oak fireplace mantel that my dad had made before I was born. It was extravagant to us, and the center of our home. My parents sold that house when I was six years old, and the mantel along with it. When I was a teenager working at MTV, making my own money, I came home for the holidays and bemoaned the tiny, flat white mantel in my parents' home.

"You wanna go to the lumber yard and make another one?" I asked my dad, and together we worked on a beautiful new mantel. The pride of re-creating that family treasure made me feel better about myself than any professional accomplishment.

A pattern ensued. Whenever I wanted to feel good about myself, I burrowed into home improvement projects. Here's one of my favorites. In the original farmhouse at Mischief Farm, the Kitchen had shitty old linoleum flooring while the whole rest of the house had original wood floors. I'd promised Jeff I wouldn't spend a lot of money fixing that place up, so I went to Home Depot and picked out six sheets of plywood. Most home improvement stores will cut the sheets for you as narrow as twelve inches. I sanded all my plywood planks and then sanded down all the edges to re-create old farmhouse flooring. I laid them out in a herringbone pattern and then did a chalk paint whitewash on them. After a few coats of matte protective polyure-thane, they were sturdy, chic, and cheap as hell.

If you're a newbie to home renovation, a few tools are must-haves. Get yourself a cordless drill. It's the tool I use most often. The drill comes with bits for everything from drilling holes to mixing paint. I'm also a huge fan of the compound miter saw. It makes projects like flooring so much quicker and much more precise. My dad gave me one for my twenty-first birthday, and it's been a game changer.

If you're looking for tools for small projects, I just recently dis-covered and really enjoy the Dremel rotary tool kit. You can cut, drill, sand, and sculpt to your heart's desire.

Every year new toys come out, but those are my standbys. I feel my prettiest with sawdust in my hair and at least one bloody knuckle.

hive case that had a glass window so you could see all the bees at work. Gus always jostled his way up through the swarm of kids. At the market Jeff radiated charm.

One gorgeous May day some really cute, shy girls were working at the poultry and egg booth, Quattro's. If you have a party up here, it's a faux pas not to serve Quattro's pheasant sausage. So, we always make it a point to stop there. In a basket of straw were huge, fist-size eggs that looked like a small dinosaur had laid them.

"What are those?" I asked.

"Wild turkey eggs," one of the girls told me. "We only have them in the month of May, and only for about two or three weeks. So if you want to try them, try them now."

At home, Jeff heated up the skillet with a little butter, and I cracked the eggs. The shells were speckled brown and much harder than the shells of chicken eggs, and the membrane that lines the shell was so tough I had to tear into it with my fingernail. Jeff fried them up, and I sliced some of the bread we'd bought. The bright yolks were smoky and rich. If chicken eggs are a McDonald's hamburger, then wild turkey eggs are a perfectly cooked filet mignon.

We went back the next weekend and bought a dozen of them, and then we ran into Pam and Roger Hoffman, of Hoffman's Barn fame, the source of my everything. Pam took me by the arm. "Oh, Hilarie, I want you to meet my son, John."

We knew John Traver, but barely. He was Ira's shy, smiling wingman at Samuel's. "Hey man, nice to see you," Jeff offered.

"John is running for town council," his mother said, beaming as John shook hands with another couple and passed out stickers and fliers.

"Well hell," Jeff said, "make us up some T-shirts, and we'll be your personal billboards."

For the Fourth of July, Jeff's old buddy Jeremy Sisto, his beautiful wife, Addie, and their two kids came out to stay at the cabin we couldn't shut up about. Jeff has known Jeremy forever; they were dudes in LA together. They grew up together. And Addie is amazing; she rides horses, and it took her about half a minute before she was encouraging our country adventure. "Yes! Live there full time," she said. "We would if we could."

Their son was just a baby, a couple of years younger than Gus, and their daughter was just a couple of years older, so those kids made a fearsome trio. Wild-haired and seldom-shoed, they were funny and spirited, and I liked their parents more for how they were raising their kids. It was very tight quarters, with bodies in beds and on couches and in sleeping bags and kids and dogs running wild. We built a fire every night and stayed up late, gossiping and hatching plans to work together or just quit everything and turn into a commune.

Jeremy invited us to a Fourth of July party at his friend Andy Ostroy's house in Rhinebeck. Andy's beautiful house cut into the side of a hill. A swimming pool skimmed the top of the hillside, and as we made our way through the gate, he and his girlfriend Phoebe greeted us with warmth and ease. Still, my default when I'm in a situation where I don't know anyone is to talk to the kids at the party, and seeing as how Gus was two years old and insane, it seemed pretty legitimate to be keeping an eye on him.

Another two-year-old was there; she was very shy, but Gus was determined that they were going to be friends and proceeded to pursue her rather aggressively. I sat on the floor, trying to keep Gus from emptying the bowl of chips, and struck up a conversation with a seven-year-old boy in cool, hipster glasses. I had no idea who he belonged to until I was introduced to his mom, Julie, who was also the mother of the little girl Gus was pursuing.

"I'm sorry my family is infiltrating yours," I said somewhat sheepishly.

Then she introduced me to her husband, Paul.

Hi Paul Rudd, I thought. *Please don't remember me. I interviewed you once at MTV during my really awkward years, and I'd like to think I'm an entirely different person now.* I felt like a creep. Did they think I was talking to their kids just to get to them? But it turned out I was overthinking it. They were perfectly kind and equally as welcoming as Andy and Phoebe had been.

The kids spent the day splashing in the pool and begging various moms for "just one more soda." As dusk was settling in, Andy called out, "Time to go to the river for fireworks. See you guys at Clermont." The Clermont State Historic Site along the Hudson River has a huge sloped property that offers perfect views of the fireworks across the river.

Julie had remembered the blanket, the bug spray, the hand wipes, and the snacks. I had brought none of these things. She was so kind and shared everything with us, and before I knew it, I had an enormous lady crush on her. "I think I'm in mom-love with her," I told Jeffrey as we drove home that night.

I saw Jules again later that summer at our friend Griffin Dunne's house, and I felt that embarrassing joy like when a senior invites you, a sophomore, to sit at their lunch table. She is such a smart woman, and she understood everything I was going through—what it was like being the mostly-stay-at-home person and having a partner with a high-profile career whom women threw themselves at—all the trappings of fame. We have both been elbowed out of the way by fans who think they have a shot with our partner, or by other actors and producers who don't waste time on "the plus ones." I'd always been so hot-headed about those situations. Julie had been a vice president at a major film studio, had a big creative career, and made all the same choices I was making, but she'd made them eight years before. Julie had navigated it all beautifully and was seemingly unstressed. I thought, *Whatever she's doing, I want to do.* Jules showed up in my life exactly when I needed her.

That group of buddies was the linchpin—Andy to debate politics and gossip about juicy current events, Phoebe to gush about theater and our love of documentaries, Paul to inject absurdity and mischief into any situation, and Jules to infuse everything with her absolute chillness. I have friends I love dearly in California. But between traffic and schedules and especially with a baby, getting together was always so inconvenient and we rarely saw each other. In Rhinebeck we started having regular Saturday dinners and lazy afternoons at each others' houses.

I began to notice that every time I went back to LA, I'd funnel more things back to the cabin.

Part Two

GROW

5

When you look for the bad, expecting it,
you will get it. When you know you will
find the good—you will get that.

—Eleanor H. Porter, *Pollyanna*

hen Gus turned three, we had to make a decision about preschool, which meant we had to finally decide whether LA or Rhinebeck was going
to be home base. Getting into school in Los Angeles isn't just
insanely competitive; it's mortal combat. We started hearing stories from friends about the interview process, about a
French immersion school where children were reading by the
time they were two years old. This was so foreign to Jeff and me.
I grew up going to preschool at the split-level house of Mrs. Ann
Allison (of Witches Brew fame) in Sterling Park not far from
ours. She lived upstairs, and downstairs we learned our ABCs
and all about Jesus. Of course, everyone wants their kids to have
more than what they had, but the idea of this little not-even-
three-year-old being interviewed, or the school looking at us
and wondering, *Are you famous enough? Do you have enough pull?
Do you have enough money?* I couldn't do it. We put our heads in
the sand.

Instead of being in LA looking at schools, or letting them look at us, we were at the cabin. The trees were budding, the forsythia bushes were boasting their beautiful yellow blooms, and the sun was out. Gus was catching turtles with his dad down by the reservoir, learning about leaves and bugs and rocks. That little boy loved rocks. It wasn't Proust, but I'd like to think the curiosity he was tapping in to was something more valuable.

One day, Jeff had a Skype meeting with a producer about a potential job. If it worked out, it would mean a little less travel for him. I wanted it to work! For the meeting, I had to get Gus out of the house because he was a loud toddler who loved to crash his Thomas trains and yell "Percy is coming!" over and over. If you aren't familiar with Thomas the Train, Percy is Thomas's buddy the little green engine. But that *particular* phrase sounds really bad when shouted by a toddler in the background of a business meeting.

I bundled him up and we headed off to the Lions Club park just down the hill from the high school and beside the brook where, I've been told, all the teenagers dangle their feet and swap their first kisses.

As we were playing, a Gus-size boy with a huge head of bright yellow curls came running over. Sam and Gus took to each other immediately, and I was left talking to Sam's dad, Paul, who within two minutes asked the million-dollar question: "Where are you going to put Gus in school?"

"I have no idea," I admitted.

"Well, over in Red Hook, there's a really cute preschool named Little Feet. It's in the old chocolate factory, and the teacher, Ms. Patty, is supposed to be amazing."

Right then I knew—we didn't have to be in LA. We could make a life here, at the cabin. Frantic, I started grilling this poor man. How big is the class size, what's the tuition, and how do I find Ms. Patty!?

An hour later Gus and I burst through the cabin door, breathless. As casual as the cat who swallowed the canary, I asked Jeff, "How was your call, babe?"

"It was great. How was the playground?"

A mile a minute, I relayed all that I had learned. I told him all about Sam and Paul and Ms. Patty, and he sat there with a dopey smile on his face. When I'd finished, or at least stopped for air, he said, "Cool. I have the number for that place. My knee surgeon, Andrew, suggested it too." Kismet.

We still had to persuade Ms. Patty to make room for Gus. Her classroom was magical and filled with the scent of patchouli, which she told me calms the kids. I don't know if we convinced her, but Gus, well, he wasn't going to leave that sweet little school until he had a promise that he could go back. And just like that, we became fulltime cabiners.

We already had the wardrobes. When you start an acting gig, you usually do your read-through and then you go to your wardrobe fitting, and that helps you take on the shape of your characters. Over the previous two years Jeff and I had shoved all our LA gear—his bracelets and rings and Chrome Hearts collection and my trinkets and hippie skirts—into boxes, and we basically only wore things that we could buy at the hardware store or at the department store in town. Only this wasn't for a role, and we weren't acting. Changing out our LA wardrobe for our Rhinebeck clothes felt natural and right.

Ira sent us to the Rhinebeck Department Store, owned by Barbara and Dick. Dick is a fox. A cashmere-sweater-collared-shirt-pressed-chinos handsome man, and I *know* that in his youth he was deadly. Barbara is his much younger wife who is a source of boundless good cheer and energy. I'd put money on her being the captain of the cheerleading squad. They saw the similar age difference between Jeff and me and felt that we were kindred spirits.

Barbara creates incredible window displays, and inside the store are old, wide-plank wood floors and a gorgeous, scraggly moose head hanging over all of the goods they carry—the kinds of things that your grandpa wears but hipsters in Brooklyn have appropriated.

We bought Pendleton blankets and wool coats and sweaters and things that will last a hundred years. Jeffrey was adamant that he and Gus have the matching red-and-black plaid one-piece jammies Barb put up in her window, complete with the button-up butt—they were both always running around with their butts hanging out of those things.

I soon learned that my skill set fit the environment at the cabin. I could knit my son a sweater. I could build myself a garden. I could do the hard-scaping and landscaping, the painting and putting together. The women in my family were very capable and made pies from scratch and plucked their own chickens. I'd heard stories of my dad's mom grabbing snakes by the tail and cracking them like whips so they couldn't bite her kids. Or my great-grandmother Alice, who was the first woman in town to bob her hair and who worked a job that was usually reserved for male employees until she had earned enough money to buy a whole farm for her tall, younger husband. As a kid, I would hang out in the kitchen with the ladies. One aunt in particular could wash the dishes with her sleeves buttoned at the wrist and not get a drop of water on herself. It was the most precise thing I'd ever seen. That was elegance! And I finally felt like I fit in with these strong women.

One evening while at dinner with the Rudds at Gaby's, a little Mexican place in town, my phone dinged with a new email.

"Ha! I just got an offer for a Christmas movie called *Naughty or Nice!*" I rolled my eyes. Jeff laughed.

"Hold the phone!" Julie said, shutting down the noise of the kids. "Tell me more!"

"Umm, the character is named Krissy Kringle," I read, laughing.

"Oh my God, you have to do it," Julie insisted.

There was zero chance I was going to do some cheese-ball Christmas movie. That was like career suicide.

"I don't think you understand. We love those movies," Jules cried.

"We *love* those movies," Paul chimed in.

"We're Jewish, and we live for Christmas movies," Julie insisted.

"Read us the synopsis," Paul demanded.

The description had every cliché, but it also sounded kind of fun. My friends were babbling on about how wonderful this was. When I told them I couldn't do it, I thought they were going to climb over the table, snatch my phone, and accept the offer for me.

Jules said, "You *have* to do it!"

Paul said, "I dare you to do it."

After that dinner, I kept thinking, *What else am I doing?*

My acting work had always been my dream. Getting a job like the one I had on *One Tree Hill* was what I had wanted for my entire life. It was a fairy tale—I was a small-town girl who at age twenty had worked at MTV and now had a great role on a new series. But have you ever read a fairy tale? I mean, an original Brothers Grimm fairy tale, like Cinderella, where the stepsister cuts off her own toe to fit her foot into the glass slipper? They are dark. And in my particular fairy tale there had been a villain who pitted female actors against one another, pushed us to do gratuitous sex scenes that always left me feeling ill and ashamed, told young female actors to stick their chests out, put his hands on all of us, and pushed himself on me, forcing unwanted kisses.

I wasn't completely naïve—when I was at *TRL* Ben Affleck had groped me on camera; I was nineteen, and I'd taken it on the chin and kept going. One of MTV's top brass called me and said, "You handled that so well." I didn't realize that I was being groomed—trained to be a good girl and *a good sport*, someone who would put up with much worse behavior.

Those experiences left me exhausted and jaded. Jeffrey helped me find my love of acting again. When I met him, he told me, "If you're going to work, I want it to be fun for you. No more taking jobs that put you in a bad place." He took all the hard shit off the table. I know not everyone is this fortunate, and I'm thankful every day.

Working on *White Collar* resurrected my love for acting. That team of creatives and professionals showed me how a production is supposed to work, based on mutual respect and deep kindness. I had minimal responsibilities there, which was perfect. But I definitely did not want to sign up for six years on another show ever again. As an actor, you go into auditions begging *please hire me*. They interview and audition you, but there's never a point where you get to sit down with the producers and ask, Okay, what's *your* track record? Are you a creep? Are you going to bring your baggage to work? You don't get to see all the cards before you have to play the game. And once Gus came along, I didn't want to take a chance like that—I could be stuck in a miserable job until he was in fifth grade. I loved to act, but I had to figure out a way to do it that worked for me.

The previous year had been a bum out, professionally. I had new goals now. I was determined to find a female-driven vehicle I could thrive in. My manager, Meg, was thrilled I was going to make a go of it and actually audition.

I pored over scripts. There was an overwhelming theme in that year's crop of pilots. Slut cops. Captains who get frisky when they're stressed. FBI agents who can't help but kiss their co-workers. These babes were women in power, but they were also DTF.

I approached these auditions like I would any job. I did some research, looked at real female officers, paid close attention to how they dressed, talked, carried themselves, wore their hair.

The feedback from casting directors was hilarious.

"What'd they say?" I asked Meg after one audition for a job I really, really, *really* wanted.

"Well honey, they said you were . . . frigid."

And another one, "They'd like to know if you could come back and change your hair and clothes."

"Change them how?"

"Edgier? 'More dangerous' is the note I got."

"So . . . slutty?"

"Exactly."

I do not exaggerate when I say this went on for dozens of auditions. I even ran into Sophia Bush in the waiting room on more than one occasion. "Can you believe this shit?" we lamented. If only they would cast us—then we could use our powers of persuasion and common sense to convince the producers that after a woman investigates a grisly murder scene and finds out her dad is the culprit, she does *not* want to take her shirt off for some dude. No matter how hard he smolders.

My plans of being a power female were going down in flames.

But then I got a call. "Remember the hot biker cop role?" Meg asked.

Yeah, I remembered. "Well, you didn't get that. But Michael Peña is the lead and he's getting a say in who plays his ex-wife, so they want you to come in and read with him."

Playing the role of a nagging, concerned ex-wife? Mother to a small son? Don't have to get naked or be sexy or brood? Wear sensible shoes? I could do that in my sleep. Michael picked me out of the lot. I don't want to brag, but my nagging is definitely Emmy worthy.

But the show didn't get picked up.

Hence my availability for the Christmas movie offer, which felt to me like a step backward. But then the producers told me that Meredith Baxter and Michael Gross, the parents from *Family Ties*, were going to play my parents. What? How cool. I couldn't say no.

When I read the script, I saw that no one was asking me to do anything inappropriate. I didn't have to take my shirt off. I didn't have to say provocative things. There was barely a kiss at the end of the movie. The shoot was only three weeks long, so I didn't even have to hire a full-time nanny. I needed only a babysitter to help me out. The idea that I could do these little tiny spurts of work that I felt good about and be a mom for the rest of the year was very appealing.

At first, I was defensive about doing these kinds of jobs—it's only three weeks, they pay women what they're worth, they don't make me take my clothes off—rather than just admitting that I liked doing them and that I also liked to crochet, garden, and watch old movies. There was so much pressure when I was in my twenties, when independent film was ascendant and everyone wanted to play a heroin addict or a sex worker, to make "art" films. But in this odd little holiday genre, I unexpectedly found my power-woman roles. I had control in casting and script changes and how my character looked and dressed. This was a revelation!

My feminist manifesto came in the form of an elf costume.

I'm interested in making art that helps an audience feel good and inspired to rise to the occasion. If I can make people comfortable enough to hear the message and be empowered, then that's good art to me.

Quickly, my favorite gigs became working for Lifetime because women are valued on those jobs. The most important player is a woman. The audience is decidedly female. The directors and writers, all women. A woman is always number one on the call sheet. So, I was happily making movies about stressed-out women living fast-paced city lives and then going to the country to find some homespun love. Sound familiar?

The first week on these jobs is always about getting to know co-workers. We ask each other the usual questions: Where do you live? What do you do on the weekends? Do you have kids? Over and over I found myself having to explain that I didn't live in California or New York. When I'd say, "I live in a log cabin and my husband chops wood to keep our house warm," I had to laugh out loud, and whomever I was talking to would inevitably say, "Oh my God, your life *is* a Christmas movie."

They weren't wrong, and I was incredibly grateful. I had never felt more supported professionally in my entire life. Paul and Jules were cheering me on. Barbara and Dick and the ladies who worked for them at the department store were over the moon that I started doing Christmas movies set in little towns just like ours.

The Christmas movies also meant I had plenty of time for Gus, but now that he was going to be in school with Ms. Patty, my days would start to become mine again, and it made sense to start trying for that second baby.

Jeff was reluctant. Gus had been a miracle baby, and he was growing into a special kid. The three of us had found a great balance, and Jeffrey was afraid of upsetting the scales. He would say, "Gus is perfect. We're perfect. It's easy to travel as a family. Let's not throw a monkey wrench into this."

I felt rejected that he didn't want to grow our family the way we'd initially planned. I hadn't signed up to have a one-kid family. I wanted to be pregnant again. I loved feeling like my body was a science experiment, and choosing natural childbirth had given me a lot of confidence. That was really empowering. Not to mention, I had found something I was good at, and it seemed crazy to do it only once. I didn't want to be greedy and ask for too much, but I desperately wanted another child.

6

You never know what you are going to
want until you see it clearly.

—Shirley Jackson,
The Haunting of Hill House

The memory of Grandma Dee Dee's pig farm loomed large
in Jeff's imagination. At a young age, he'd camp there
for the summer, sleeping in an old airstream trailer in
the middle of a field. Grandma's right-hand man, Clem, would
grunt at him from time to time and make sure Jeff was flush
with potatoes, which he baked over his little campfire. He was
Huck Finn, independent and curious. The farm fed that. Now
that Gus was getting older, he wanted those things for his son.

"We need a hundred acres," Jeff would say. "Get some goats.
Pigs. Cows. Let Gus sleep in the middle of the fields like I used to
do at Grandma D's house."

I loved the idea of having land where I could grow Gus his food,
raise animals, and be more self-sufficient. And wanting a bigger
house with more bedrooms seemed like a very good sign that Jeff
was warming up to adding to our family.

We started putting the word out that we were interested in buying a farm.

Connie, our favorite no-bullshit waitress at Pete's Diner, got involved. Jeff and I always sat in her section. I'd get the Western omelet, Jeff was a devotee of the Eggs Benedict, and before we even ordered Connie would come to the table with Gus's favorite hash browns, a ton of ketchup, and a bowl of fruit. So when Connie found out we were looking, she encouraged us to check out a house on the main drag that looked like something out of *The Godfather*. Large iron gates and overdone stonework shadowed the driveway. We were grateful for her help but were looking for something a little more . . . subtle.

Over at the Rhinebeck Department Store, Dick and Barbara caught wind of our quest. "Come over!" they insisted. They were getting ready to downsize from their historic home on a chunk of land to a townhouse in the Village. It wasn't even on the market yet, but as we rolled down their serene driveway past the fenced-in pastures, the daydreams kicked in. I liked the narrative of our sweet friends passing down their wonderfully curated historic home so that another family—ours—could grow and make memories in the space. The main room had a large fireplace and bookshelves for my obsessive collection. It was charming and warm. But it had many, many levels, as older homes tend to do. Back in the day, the kitchen was usually an entirely separate building. So little hallways and odd nooks filled in the gaps. Attics got turned into loft bedrooms. Additions were tacked on here and there. With a little dude who was barely walking—or for the kids I was hoping to have—it was worrisome.

When we walked into Samuel's, I'd holler, "Hiya handsome!" And if Ira had seen me coming, he'd hand me a freshly made hot mocha (since I'm a child and basically like adult hot chocolate), and John Traver, who had started working with Ira when he was fifteen and was now a store manager, would quietly smile and ask Gus what he felt like having. Then Ira would lean out the doorway of his office at the back of the shop as we leaned across the counter and talk to Jeff and me about all the boring stuff we needed to know, like which area had better water or what the politics were like in each small town. "The Red Hook schools are better at sports, and the Rhinebeck schools have more arts programs."

Then he'd whisper conspiratorially, "But really, you should come over by where my husband and I live." Ira was adamant that we move to Milan, which is pronounced *My*-lan, and if you say it the wrong way, you might as well put up a neon sign saying I'M NOT FROM HERE. Milan was close to Gus's preschool, which was appealing. But on top of that, Ira painted a picture of dinner parties and evening strolls and plenty of rolling green acreage to keep us busy. We quickly started trolling the real estate websites for Milan listings.

Ira was very protective of our family. One summer day we had been milling about the coffee shop gabbing with Ira and John. After falling in love with the St. James Cheese Company during all his time filming in New Orleans, Jeffrey was sharing his daydream with Ira and plotting about having a sweet shop *and* a savory shop.

John was giving Gus and me a "sample" of Celeste's bark, as if we hadn't each eaten about a ton of it over the previous two years, when a woman walked into the store and recognized Jeffrey and then started whipping out her phone before announcing that we had to take a picture.

Jeffrey and I have always been people pleasers; we never want to hurt anybody's feelings, but we were also extremely protective of Gus. Even so, saying "no" was hard. But Ira swooped between the camera and me, and in his frank but gracious way said, "Please, this is their family time. They moved here because they want to avoid all that."

Ira understood us deeply and wanted only our friendship. In the years we'd known him, it would have done his shop so much good if he had posted a picture of us on his website, but he never asked for anything—not an autograph or selfie or endorsement of any kind. Ira's friendship was a balm for Jeffrey. Most people just wanted to talk to Jeffrey about work, but Ira wanted to talk about cheese and chocolate and property.

We kept looking, hoping to find something in Milan. We found a log cabin on a deep slope of acreage that had a guesthouse and its own nine-hole golf course and a basement designed for a serious prepper. But it was forty-five minutes from Rhinebeck, and we didn't want to be that far from our friends, so we kept looking.

Then one day Ira called and told us, "There's an old farm very close to my place. It's gorgeous! You have to come see it right away."

My stomach fluttered as we drove up the driveway to a beautiful eighteenth-century light-blue farmhouse with a huge party barn where the owner had been hosting weddings. Pathways of slate connected the barns, the guesthouse, and the main house. The original portion of the home was paneled in ancient wood, and fireplaces graced every room. A huge, tasteful addition had been built, creating a thousand-square-foot bonus room for toys. You know how many Thomas the Train tracks you can fit into a room that size?

The woman selling the place was a beekeeper, and besides the apiary she had goats and sheep and cows here and there. I looked out an upstairs window across her rocky fields and thought of my teenage obsession, *Wuthering Heights*. It was craggy land with animals roaming all over the place and no neighbors in sight. And Jeffrey had always been a bit of a Heathcliff (probably what I was attracted to). I could see the next twenty years of our lives unfolding across those fields.

But it turned out that years before, someone had given a right-of-way, an easement, to a local farmer so he could feed his cattle, which meant that there was a public thoroughfare through the middle of the property, right up to the kitchen window of the home, where strangers and stalkers could show up at any time.

When our agent, Rick, called me with the news, I felt like a child—my eyes stung, my throat ached, and I chewed on my lip trying not to cry. We consulted lawyers. I spent countless hours on the phone with my mother—a very successful real estate agent—trying to find a way around this obstacle. But it was no use. The blue house on the hill just wasn't going to work.

I was devastated. I drove by that house after school drop-off for a solid week.

One October morning Rick called me. He was at a brokers' open house on a horse farm that was going on the market. "You need to get in your car and get over here now because there's going to be multiple offers." His voice was electric.

"Jeff, Gus, we've gotta go," I called out into the cabin unnecessarily loudly, given that we were all sitting within three feet of one another.

I hurriedly put a blue striped sweater under Gus's toddler over-alls and thrust his feet into his boots. We threw ourselves into the car, and fifteen minutes later we were pulling up a long gravel driveway that sliced through a sea of Kentucky bluegrass flown in by the owners for their horses. The original farmhouse, which was built in the late 1800s, was tucked away on the left, and at the top of the hill we could see a newer, one-story timber-frame home.

I looked over at Jeffrey and could see it in him right away. We hadn't even gotten out of the car before he said, "This is it."

Sitting right in the front yard was a huge tom turkey. Fearless, Gus got out of the car and ran to the bird, which was as big as him, and started to follow the turkey around.

All these buildings, all this land. It was gorgeous, but it was also intimidating. Because of Jeff's work and travel schedule, I did most of the housework at the cabin by myself, so this looked like a lot of work to me. But it was one of those beautiful autumn days when the trees are flaming orange and red against a bright blue sky. From the top of the hill you could see 360 degrees in all directions. I felt like Julie Andrews up in the Alps at the beginning of *The Sound of Music*. I kept turning in every direction, and everywhere I looked there was a different story—the barns with the animals coming and going as they pleased; way off in the distance the steeple of an old church; and all around, trees and sky.

We were all in.

The owner, Sunny, and her lovely husband were at the open house. The farm had been their part-time place where Sunny had kept her horses and the family had celebrated holidays and enjoyed vacations. Now, they were trading it in to travel the world together. All the local brokers were there too. Ed Hackett, who runs the farm supply store and moonlights as a broker, was texting his client, Amar'e Stoudemire, who was playing for the Knicks and wanted a weekend retreat.

We whirled in and took over. We said hi to Rick and then honed in on the listing agent. She had lived in the community her whole life, and her father had kept cows on this property. We walked along the three miles of fence, rode in a four-wheeler down to the tree line, and crawled through the woods to see the old stone walls that mark the property lines. Gus was on a tear; he wanted to get into everything. Sunny had grandkids who were the same age as Gus, and I think she and her family were excited by the thought of continued family life in the house.

Then we went down to the original farmhouse. Outside of the little white house were gardens that had been there since the 1930s or 1940s. The trees alongside the house were enormous old catalpa trees. Under one of them we found two headstones.

Growing up in Virginia I was used to seeing family cemeteries surrounded by wrought-iron fences in antiquated front yards. Everyone keeps their people as close as possible. You don't have to go far to visit Grandma, Great-Grandma, and Great-Great-Grandpa—they're right out by the mailbox. For a moment I was worried that people were buried in what would be *my* yard. But then Jeff crouched down and touched the hand-carved stones. The one on the left read *Mischief, 1936 to 1950*; the one on the right read *Mischief 2, 1951 to 1960*. "The man who built the farm was a cat lover," the listing agent told us. I ran my fingers along the chisel marks he'd made so many years ago.

Sunny, Tom the turkey, and the family's little dog walked us to our truck. We hugged Sunny goodbye and warmly pressed the hand of the listing agent; then, as they walked away, we had a huddle with Rick that went something like this:

Jeff: We're gonna buy this house. We'll give them full ask. (Rick opened his mouth to speak.)

Me: We're all gonna drive away right now. Rick, let's do whatever we gotta do to get our offer in within the hour.

Rick: Okay.

We weren't playing hardball. We wanted it. We were ready for it. I don't think Sunny ever even had other people go through the house.

As we got into the car to drive back to the cabin, I said to Jeff, "Should we call it Mischief Farm?"

He smiled. There was just no other name for it. It was always going to be that.

7

His answer to every problem, every setback
was "I will work harder!"—which he had
adopted as his personal motto.

—**George Orwell,** *Animal Farm*

One condition Sunny had before she would accept the
offer was that we had to go over for lunch at the house.
We had to prove that we weren't going to buy her home
and then destroy it. Sunny needed to know that whoever took
over the farm was going to treat the place well. We met Sunny's
children and grandchildren, her neighbors, and the farm employees. Once she got a sense that we really loved the farm for
the same reasons she did, she took me under her wing.

We passed our vetting in October but couldn't move in until
January; the family wanted one last Christmas in the house, which
I understood—but man, those few months were agonizing. The
farm was fifteen minutes from the cabin, so Jeff and I would drop
Gus off at school and drive by the farm real slow, talking about all
the things we wanted to do.

My number one priority was a garden. In high school I'd tried
tending a garden but had failed because I was set on weird things
and I didn't care whether they were meant to be grown in Virginia

or South America. I was finally adult enough to realize I should probably look up what grows well where I was living. I spent the whole winter obsessively hunched over my pad of graph paper figuring out what was going to go where, looking up Native American ways of planting. I wanted to feel the ceremony of working with the earth and practice firsthand what I'd only read about in college. There's a method of companion planting called the three sisters where you plant corn, squash, and beans together and they hold each other up. I kept a pile of inspiringly illustrated gardening books that I bought at Oblong Books & Music. I would go in there once a week and chat with whatever lovely person was at the counter, and they'd walk me over to the local section and pull out whatever I needed.

Once I'd plotted the garden, I moved on to alpacas. Yep, you read that right. In a million years I never would have guessed that we'd be alpaca farmers, but here we were. The horses all got sent to live on the neighboring farms of Sunny's friends and fellow breeders, but she knew it was going to be difficult to board her three alpacas (and one llama). "How would you feel about boarding them for me?" she asked.

There's a scene in the Barbra Streisand movie *Funny Girl* where her character is desperately trying to make it in the vaudeville circuit. After consistent rejection, someone at the theater asks her, "Can you roller skate?" And she responds with all the bravado in the world, "Can *I* roller skate!" In the next scene we see her bust her ass over and over, toppling all the other showgirls around her, but that isn't what matters! She was onstage. She was doing it. Failure be damned, she was living the dream. When Sunny asked whether I'd take the alpacas, that scene came rushing back to me.

(Side note: That scene is how I approach 99 percent of my life. Motherhood. Home renovations. Cooking dinner. You just gotta go in thinking, "Of course I can do this!")

"Yes. Of course. I'd love to. I can totally handle that." Followed by a frantic "Hey Jeff, we're good taking the alpacas, yeah?"

He was pumped. It was like getting a turnkey farm. I would be able to learn with animals that were already comfortable in their home and their routine. Sunny walked me through how to give them their deworming shots once a month, and I went to school on alpacas. I learned that, thankfully, they are the least-high-maintenance animals on the planet. They just nibble the tops of grass, like lanky, fluffy, roving lawnmowers. Goats and sheep look very cute, but they can destroy pastureland because they eat grass by pulling it up from the roots. And they have hooves, which tear up everything. The ever-accommodating alpacas and llama don't have hooves; they have padded feet like dogs so they don't tear the grass. You know what's even cooler? They don't poop all over the pasture; they have a "communal pile," where they do their business. Honestly, if I needed to choose a barnyard animal to be my roommate in college, the alpaca would win, hands down.

This was getting exciting.

It was a no-brainer that our dream farm included chickens. In all the fancy-pants grocery stores I had ever gone to, brown eggs were always the top of the egg hierarchy. Words like "free range" and "organic" made me feel like I wasn't just paying more for eggs; I was pitching in to ensure a beautiful life for those hardworking lady birds. So when Sunny explained that her birds laid Easter-colored eggs, I was awestruck. *That was a real thing?* I learned that different chicken breeds lay different-colored eggs, and the color

Gardening Gloves Are for Sissies

My mother always had a beautiful garden while we were growing up. Gardening seemed to come naturally to her. I took it for granted that she knew exactly how to plant things so that something would be blooming from spring to fall. (Now I know just how difficult all that planning is!) Her vegetables were orderly. Her flowers were tallest in the back and daintiest up front. Her garden always looked like something out of *Better Homes and Gardens*.

We grew all kinds of things—corn, cucumbers, strawberries, tomatoes, and snow peas. My younger brother John would hunch down by the bushes of beans, popping them in his mouth. We thought nothing of wandering barefoot into Mom's lovely little corner of the world, grabbing at tomatoes and whatever else was ripe with one hand while holding on to the long green hose with the other, fighting over turns at drinking that delicious metallic water. She was a good sport about it. At least it meant she wouldn't have to fix us lunch.

Here are a few tricks I've learned to help my garden grow:

* To get rid of slugs, break up your eggshells and place the shards in a ring around your plants. To slugs, it's like crawling across broken glass.

* Put marigolds around vegetable plants to keep away pests such as destructive insects and wild rabbits. When the flowers dry out, harvest the seeds by plucking the flower head and placing it in a paper bag, where it can dry completely. These make great

gifts for teachers and friends. We call them Mischief Farm Marigolds.

* I always refuse to thin out carrots. You're supposed to thin them out so they grow long and thin and deep. But at Mischief Farm, we get twisty carrots that look like monsters. I'm not sure whether that's a tip or a failure, but either way, we love the carrot creatures we grow each year, and I wouldn't do it any other way. Give it a try!

* If birds or dogs or wild animals are digging up your garden, pick up a bunch of cayenne pepper. My grocery store carries big containers in the international food aisle. Sprinkle pepper all over the dirt. It won't hurt the plants and it won't hurt the animals, but they'll think twice about digging in your garden.

* I learned the importance of rotating crops from my mom. Every year or so, her farming relatives in Iowa would flip-flop the corn and soybean fields so as not to overtax the soil nutrients. When my mother visited, she and other kids would be assigned the chore of "walking the beans," which meant walking along the bean rows to make sure no corn was popping up. She made it sound like the coolest task a kid could do. On a much smaller scale we practice the same thing in our garden, rotating the crops every year so that each plant gets the nutrients it needs and the soil can replenish itself.

of the egg is largely dependent on what color the chicken's feet are. If you have a bird that has darker colored feathers and orange feet, it will lay brown eggs. There are chickens that have blue feet, and they lay blue eggs; and the green-footed ones lay green eggs.

Sunny took her chickens and turkey with her to Westchester, and we planned on getting our own chicks from the feed store in the spring. But after a week in Westchester, a military-like attack from the local raccoons saw the chickens' numbers dwindle. Sunny texted, Hilarie, I can't keep the chickens here. Do you guys want them?

Yes. So much yes.

One toddler, two dogs, three alpacas, one llama, seventeen chickens, and a seventy-acre farm seemed like a lot. We were also carrying three mortgages, which was daunting, and Jeff didn't want to give up our magical cabin. He insisted on keeping it, as impractical as that was. "There aren't a lot of woods at the farm," he'd reason. "I need to be able to come back and chop firewood." Uh huh. He just had his grownup playhouse that he had always wanted. It was too magical to give up, so we started letting friends from the city come up and use it. Time and time again, everyone commented on how much love was in that tiny log hideout.

That left the LA house. Jeff made a casual call to his agent in California, asked her what she thought the house might be worth, and told her to let us know if she knew of anyone who was interested. The house didn't sit on the market. After the first brokers' open house, offers flooded in. We were a bit shocked at the speed of everything, but thankfully Nick, who had been housesitting for us, helped us deal with the real estate agent; gave tours of the home to buyers, using his theatrical flair to really sell the place; oversaw repairs; and packed up most of our belongings. When I flew in, he helped me settle the last lot of stuff.

I was unexpectedly weepy saying goodbye to that house. The bar where Jeff and I had flirted and traded numbers. The corner where the Christmas tree had stood when he proposed. The pool where Gus had learned to swim. The office where I had labored. The nail holes where the deer head had once hung. Shit, this was sad! Nick and I were about to get in the car when I ran to the backyard and picked every lemon off the tree.

As I was clambering into the car, one of the neighbors I had met multiple times came outside and said, "Oh, hi. Are you two the new neighbors?"

Never mind. I couldn't get back to the cabin fast enough.

In Rhinebeck the weather was changing. We had just spent Thanksgiving at the Rudds' house with Julie's dad, who spoiled the kids with little gifts and played on the floor with them. The Saturday after, I woke up to a carpet of frost around the cabin. Gus and I dehydrated lemon wedges in the oven, covered them in Mod Podge, and made a lemon garland that we strung on our Christmas tree.

That night, Jeff, Gus, and I bundled up and went into town for the Sinterklaas festival. I had ordered gift boxes of candy for all the people we work with, and so we stopped by Samuel's to settle up. Ira had meticulously made perfect packages. The shop twinkled with white Christmas lights, and garland ran along the high shelves that displayed Ira's artifacts—tin soldiers, vintage lunchboxes, birdhouses made by talented locals. A huge old stereo from the early 1990s took up an obscene amount of space on top of the milk cooler behind the register. Elvis and Bing and Burl Ives all crooned. People were crammed into every nook of the store, buying gifts and something warm to drink.

"Hiya handsome," I called out to Ira.

"Boxes are sent, doll! Jeff, I saw your wife kissing Tyler Hilton!" Ira teased me about the promos for my latest holiday movie. He was obsessed with Christmas and never missed one of my movies.

"That kid's a prince," Jeff responded. "I'd kiss him too."

"How are you holding up?" I asked him, the madness of the store causing us to shout a bit.

"Exhausted! Packed a hundred mail-order boxes last night, slept for an hour, and then came back here for the Teddy Bear Beauty Pageant." Ira held up his own rust-colored bear that had been camped out by the register. Ira's Teddy Bear Beauty Pageant was legendary. All the children in town would doll up their bears in costumes made from old baby clothes, discarded Halloween accessories, paper towel rolls, and Mardi Gras beads. Ira bestowed a special title on each one of them. "I pronounce this the Rock 'n Roll Gladiator Bear!" or "Let's hear it for the Sugar Plum Princess Bear!" Then each kid was gifted a shiny foil-wrapped chocolate bear for their efforts. "Gus! You gonna come dress up a bear for me next year?" Gus feigned shyness and buried his head in my legs.

I handed Ira a little box. I'd been doing my Christmas shopping at Paper Trail, my favorite stationery store in Rhinebeck, and I'd found a gorgeous glass fox ornament, dusted in snowy crystals. The raised eyebrows of the creature reminded me of my mischievous friend. Handing it over to him, I watched as Ira read the card: "To Ira, You're a Stone Fox! So grateful for you and your friendship." He cocked a clever eyebrow and held up the glass fox. Then he went back into the storage room and pulled out a box wrapped in shiny silver paper. Gus tore the giftwrap and found a collection of Dr. Seuss books, his first, and threw his arms around Ira's legs.

I grabbed Ira and kissed his face, and then he was pulled back into the fray of hot chocolate and candy canes.

A few doors down, at Pete's Diner, we delivered a gift to Connie. For someone with such a gruff front, she is wonderfully kind-hearted. She gives us a Christmas card every year, knits us scarves, remembers every birthday, and every time she goes on vacation in Maine, she brings me back a calendar.

Then we headed to Osaka, the sushi restaurant in town, to grab a bite with Andy, Phoebe, and the Rudds before the festival began. The waitress, Sarah, knows what food and drink all of our kids prefer. She knows what special Jeff wants to order before he even asks for it. She is maternal and wonderful and has fed my boys dinner multiple nights in a row whenever I've been off working in the city. Jass and her husband, John, who run the restaurant with Jass's parents, came out to greet us and wish us a happy Sinterklaas.

As it started to get dark, the street filled up and we all headed over to Samuel's, where Ira ushered us up onto his bench. The sea of people moved this way and that as each new float and group of performers and huge puppet display moved down the street.

This was Gus's first year in preschool, and when he looked up and saw Ms. Patty in her crazy costume—part Joseph's amazing Technicolor dream coat and part a costume from *The Wiz*—well, you would have thought he'd spotted Elvis. From atop Jeff's shoulders he clapped his hands and screeched, "Ms. Patty! Ms. Patty!" and when she turned in our direction, I thought he might faint from the excitement.

After the parade the town tree stood lit up in the municipal parking lot, a gathering place for locals. Gus ran into some kids from school, and he was so excited to be with *his* people, rather than folks mom and dad were introducing him to.

A few days later I was curled up on the couch in front of the fire at the cabin. Ira emailed me after he had rewatched my latest holiday movie. It was lovely and warm and totally Ira. He wrote that it was "fantastic watching you knowing I get a hug next time I see you." Ira knew he got me in real life, and that was the truth. He signed it, "Big hugs & kisses right back at you." Reading it, I grinned.

The New Year kicked off our new adventure at Mischief Farm. And naturally, not a damn thing went according to plan. Except the Seahawks winning the Super Bowl. That alone saved our sanity.

Since we had sold the house in LA, we had everything in storage containers that were being delivered to the farm in late January, so once I got the keys to the place, I dropped Gus off at school every day and raced over to maniacally paint the new house. I ferried stuff from the cabin to the farmhouse, made sure we had food for the animals Sunny was leaving with us, and found a man with a snow plow to put on speed dial.

I was fretting about how California movers were going to navigate the arctic conditions. In January everything is frozen hard in the Hudson River Valley, and at the cabin there is always eight feet of snow.

But the day before the movers came, we had a warm spell and all of the ice and snow melted. I arrived early at the farm to unlock the house and realized I had to move my Suburban to make way for the two massive tractor trailers that were lingering at the end of the driveway. Jeffrey had told me that the driveway went past the house and back down toward the woods, then looped around, so I figured I could loop around down there and be out of the way. I drove down the fairly steep hill, and the Suburban started to wiggle from side to side. The whole hill was a layer of slick, deep mud. There was no way to turn around. *Okay,* I told myself, *I'm just going to keep going.* Problem was, I hadn't walked the perimeter of the property since that first tour at the brokers' open, so I seriously underestimated just how far I had to go. All of a sudden I was up to my eyeballs in mud.

The only way to get the Suburban out of the low-lying wetland was to try to drive it around the perimeter of the entire farm between the fencing and the tree line, which was maybe seven feet at its widest. All the frost had melted, and the ground was slicker than pig shit. I was painfully careful as I drove, white knuckles on the wheel. Every breath was a prayer. I hadn't hit a fence or bumped a tree yet, but I was leaving huge, ugly tire marks all over our brand-new farm. "Tire marks" might be too kind; really, I was tearing knee-deep trenches into the earth.

Finally, the barn appeared in the distance. I'd done it. Almost. I'd driven three-quarters of the way around the farm, but the final hill was taunting me. I'd move up a few feet, back tires swaying from side to side, and then I'd slip back, wheels spinning, sending

On Manure

Alpacas are beautiful, thoughtful animals. With their big eyes and minky long lashes, they are the J.Lo of animals, the perfect mixture of aloof and alluring. Also, their shit is pretty much the gold standard of manure, so I hoard it and dole it out sparingly for garden beds.

Great manure is farm science. When I was growing up, my family started getting horse manure from one of my dad's sisters. That stuff burns your plants and the roots unless it cures for more than six months. Horses have only one stomach chamber, so the waste isn't as broken down as in ruminants, such as cows, that have stomachs with four compartments. The seeds of unwanted weeds can pass through a horse entirely intact.

Then there's cow manure. Cows' gut bacteria is actually good for your garden, but it releases nutrients at a pretty slow pace and is lower on the nitrogen-phosphoric acid-potash scale that poop is judged on. That was my fertilizer of choice at my haunted house in North Carolina, where I'd load my 1986 gold Mercedes with as many bags of Black Gold Compost from Home Depot as the trunk could handle.

Alpacas have three stomach chambers—the magic number—and so by the time the manure comes out, it has been so processed that it contains no riff-raff seeds and is still high in nutrients. Their poop is just teeny little pellets that dry out, so they're lightweight and odor free. The crème de la crème. I daydream about my next career: Manure Sommelier.

sprays of mud into the air. There was nothing I could do to get up that last hundred yards that remained.

I scrambled out of the car and squelched my way to the barn. Sunny had encouraged us to keep on her groundskeeper, an intensely hardworking and private man (who would prefer to remain nameless, so I'll just call him Awesome). This is the man who according to legend removed briars of wild rose bushes from the entire property with just hand tools. He was tough and quiet, and I was looking forward to working with him and learning a thing or two. And now here I was destroying the beautiful paths he'd created and getting stuck in the mud before we'd moved a single box inside.

As I tried to explain the mess I'd made and how sorry I was, Awesome just raised his eyebrows. Humiliated, I had to walk him back to my car to show him exactly what was going on. When he realized what I had done, a look of horror stretched across his face, and I just knew that he was thinking, *What idiot bought this house?* But, bless him, he just turned and got the John Deere tractor and a chain and pulled me out. I left the Suburban at the barn.

Later in the day, when Jeff showed up, he asked, "You parked at the barn?"

"Oh yeah. I moved for the trucks," I said, not mentioning that I had destroyed the back forty in the process.

As we wrapped up the move from the cabin, the last order of business was to take our deer heads down. Don't worry, Jeff and I don't kill anything; we're far too sentimental for that. But Jeffrey had picked through various antique stores, rescuing any sad-faced mounts that needed a home. Not all of these creatures were grateful. One deer with a hefty set of antlers decided to exact his revenge on me for hanging him on our wall; as I pulled him down, his antlers twisted, and he snapped my hand. Gus was playing on a nearby couch when I cursed, loudly and with flourish. "You okay, mama?"

"Yup. Mama is just fine!" Jeff was out of town, Gus was still a little dude, and there was too much to do to stop and go to the ER. I walked around for four days still unpacking and setting up shop, and every time I moved a box or grabbed a paintbrush, a barbed ache beat its way from my fingers to my brain. My hand was gnarled, like I had some kind of terrible palsy.

Finally, I went to urgent care, where a doctor took x-rays and promptly told me, "Lady, you broke two bones in your hand." Cool.

We moved in to Mischief Farm, and Gus and I were promptly knocked out by a vicious flu. Jeffrey lit fires for us in the living room, but I was starting to wonder whether too many bad omens were presenting themselves. Things weren't supposed to be this hard. Nowhere in any of my beautifully illustrated farm books did they talk about broken bones and fevers and a very messy learning curve.

"This feels like the Oregon Trail. We got caught with an illness and the oxen are dying," I joked to Jeff.

"Sure, but we get three hundred points for being farmers."

It doesn't matter what you do . . . so long as you change something from the way it was before you touched it into something that's like you after you take your hands away.

—Ray Bradbury, *Fahrenheit 451*

At Mischief Farm, there were a number of projects to jump right into. The convergence of all of the various chapters of our lives was overwhelming. Everything from Jeff's LA house, all the leftovers from my North Carolina house, and all of our combined accumulations from the cabin made for one hell of an organization project. But the farm really did symbolize a commitment. No more "his" and "hers." If we were going to tackle this beast, we'd have to do it together.

In March, Jeffrey's mom and stepdad visited for Gus's fourth birthday, and I went all-out making sure that all the planters had flowers in them, everything was shipshape, and the house was spectacular. (Though two weeks later, everything I had planted died, which is when I learned that you do not plant things until after Mother's Day, even if the weather seems to have turned. The temperature *will* drop. It *will* snow. Everything *will* be destroyed. Everything.)

Jeff was out exploring one sunny day, and when he found me in the kitchen later he asked, "I found these huge divots along the perimeter of the property. Do you know what that's about?"

It was then that I had to admit my muddy moving-day debacle. "There was nothing else I could do," I said. "I had to just plow through the mud." (I think that's probably a metaphor for how we handle most things around here.)

I couldn't tell what Jeff was thinking; he had a quizzical look on his face. Finally he said, "You're a terrible driver, so I can't for the life of me understand how you drove that big-ass car through that tiny space between the fences and fucking three-hundred-year-old trees and didn't hit a thing!"

It was the highest compliment.

For Gus's birthday, we all took a trip to Ed Hackett's feed store, since the chicks arrive there every March. Gus plopped a flock of different-colored baby chicks in a box, and we kept them in our bathtub for a couple of weeks while trying to keep Bisou and Bandit from eating them. Bandit always was a little wild. He was born in the Puerto Rican jungle. Jeff had been filming there when a puppy came out of the trees and got hit by a car. Jeff insisted that he would pay the bill if somebody could get the puppy to a vet. A month later, the dog was released from the vet, in a full body cast, and someone brought him to Jeff saying, "Mr. Morgan, here's your dog." When I arrived, he sheepishly said, "So, I've got a dog. We can give it to someone else if you don't want it."

"Jeff, it's a fucking feral dog. No, I don't want it. It's going to eat our baby! You could've brought a coyote home." But Jeff is an optimist, and he had already decided in his heart that we were going to keep that dog. Feral or not, Bandit never ate a baby, human or chicken.

As an homage to the Super Bowl champions, we named the two chicks that had fluffy feet Russell Wilson and Dickie Sherman. Another was a red chicken named Red that I really loved; she was such a good layer. Another chick's beak was crooked, so she had a hard time eating; Jeff and I fed her with a dropper and trimmed her beak when needed. Gus named her Scissor Beak. Another had a head like a hawk, thus the name Hawk.

We didn't know any of the breeds. People would ask us, "Are those Leghorn Rhode Island Reds or Red Barons?"

"I don't freaking know," I'd say. "They're just cool. Gus picked them out. Gus wanted a brown one and a yellow one and a red one."

Gus became very attached to these birds. When they were pullets—two months old, not full-grown chickens, but teenagers—I took little Russell Wilson to his classroom for show-and-tell, and that chick just sat on Gus's shoulder. Nowadays, when Gus disappears, nine times out of ten he's down in the chicken houses.

After Jeff's parents left, we invited friends up to the farm for the first time to celebrate Gus's birthday. We made eggs from the bounty that Sunny's grown chickens gave us and showed off our baby chicks while Bandit sat outside the bathroom with a string of drool leaking out of his mouth.

Our dogs never tried to hurt the chickens, but other predators lurked around the farm. During that first year, there were many nights that I was frightened. At first I was scared of the coyotes. You could hear them howling into the night; it sounded like forty-seven of them were right outside the back door. That winter we also found bobcat and bear tracks in the woods.

I always watched a lot of *Dateline*, and at night in the dark with no one around, I'd scurry nervously from the car to the house, no matter how irrational it was. One night Jeff and I were lying in bed watching *The Killing* when we heard a woman screaming bloody murder. Clearly, someone was being murdered in the woods! But we didn't call 911; instead, I googled "woman screaming in woods." The first thing that came up was "female fox in heat."

You can't leave this place for five minutes without foxes getting comfortable. Once, after we'd been gone for two weeks, I was chopping tomatoes in the kitchen when I looked up and saw Bandit walking across the back deck. I couldn't understand how he had gotten outside. Then I looked closer and realized that it wasn't Bandit but a huge red fox. Our surviving rooster and hens are impressive specimens. The weak ones have been weeded out, and the ones that are still with us can literally outwit a fox.

After Gus's birthday celebrations were over, it was time to really get to work to settle into the new place. I painted and repaired the chicken houses for Sunny's brood and the new chicks. There were a couple of projects that Jeffrey wanted done right away in order to feel fully at home. For instance, the entire place was in dire need of a thick coat of paint. The exterior walls of all the barns and the house were beige with dark-green trim. It was handsome, but it wasn't us. Jeff wanted a vivid Americana fantasy farm. Lots of red and white and deep dark blue. Classic and totally something out of

Hollywood set dressing. You can take the actor out of the drama, but you can't take the drama out of the actor.

Paint did wonders for most of the buildings, but the original farmhouse was in shambles, and no amount of paint was going to fix that pit. The tenant who had lived in it for a decade never cleaned, never dusted, never repaired anything. So we inherited an avalanche of problems. Jeff wanted to just tear it down or torch it. I'd smile and nod, but I knew neither of those things was going to happen. I was in love with the house where the Mischief cats had lived, and I knew I was going to be the princess who kissed that frog and transformed it.

"Just promise me that you're not gonna waste all your time on that old dump," Jeff would say. "There's plenty of real work that needs to be done around here."

True. But now that I didn't have my old haunted house in North Carolina, this "dump" became my grownup tree house.

That spring, in the two short months we had lived at the farm, Jeff continued to get job offers that would take him far, far away. I figured I would wait till he was gone and *surprise* him. Cuz that always works, right?

I repaired the walls. All the original wood floors had been painted a clinical beige, so I rented a sander to restore them. I ripped out all the cabinets and put in new cabinetry and appliances. Although I can't run wires, I can install a new electrical fixture. The challenge in the farmhouse was that the wiring was from the 1930s—old, corroded copper wires wrapped in cloth—so I toiled with visions of electrocuting myself drifting through my brain.

While I worked, Gus sat at the picnic table outside and colored or played with cars or Thomas the Train. I set up a teepee in the yard where he stowed all his toys, and he'd run into the house from time to time to tell me what he was up to. It felt nice to know he had some freedom here. I felt fairly certain that he could run around our seventy acres and he wouldn't kill himself.

Before we'd even moved in, Sunny started sending me emails about how to take care of the property and who to go to in town to, for instance, get a fence built. She gave me a whole notebook full of resources—a guy who could do the septic work, someone who knew about chickens. One of the major resources she shared with us was the store where we'd bought the chicks, Hackett Farm Supply, which is the local resource for all your farming needs—seeds, equipment, and muck boots. Whatever you need to be a farmer, you can find it at Hackett, so naturally, Jeffrey and I overzealously started going there all the time.

Ed Hackett is one of those men who will talk shit to you until he figures out that you're someone he can trust. He's a button pusher, and he reminded me of guys who would come around when I was younger—guys my dad would coach Little League with or who had served in the military with him. Good guys who aren't intimidated by anything and will tell you to fuck off as fast as they'll say hello.

When we started shopping there, everyone gave us side-eye. I was pretty sure I could hear them thinking, *Who are these city idiots who bought Sunny's farm?* But Jeffrey and Ed quickly started getting along. We'd be nosing around the aisles looking for work gloves, and Ed would tell him, "Hey, you know what you need for the farm? You need a feeding trough." Or, "What are those boots you're wearing? You've got to try these." I was raised to be wary of salesmen, but Jeffrey was so excited to be living the farm life that he bought one of everything.

One day, Jeffrey came back from the feed store excited, saying, "Hey, I told Ed that you wanted a female alpaca, and he has two!"

"Really? He's got two?" My radar was up. I had decided I wanted to get a girl alpaca and was looking for free animals on Craigslist. There had been a big alpaca boom, and a lot of retired people had purchased them as an investment pet because the fiber is highly desirable for being hypoallergenic and softer than cashmere. And they'd get an agricultural tax exemption. But those people were getting older, and they didn't want to deal with the upkeep of the animals. So they were literally giving away alpacas that they had spent thousands of dollars on.

Jeff continued. "Yeah and they're only six hundred each, honey. Twelve hundred bucks, easy peasy."

I was listening to Jeff, thinking, *Ed! That snake oil salesman!*

We went back to the feed store the next day to get dog food. Ed came over, his blue eyes alight. "So Hilarie, I hear you want a couple girl alpacas."

I looked him in the eye. "I don't want your dirty alpacas. I'll get my own animals. I know what you're up to."

When we got in the car, Jeff just stared at me, mortified. "Why were you so rude?"

"Jeffrey, I grew up around this shit. He's not going to respect you if you just keep pulling out your credit card."

Jeffrey went back an hour later and apologized, but he shouldn't have bothered. Ed delighted in it. Ed Hackett doesn't like sissies. I had to prove to him that I wasn't a sissy.

After that, whenever I walked into the store, Ed would announce, "You're the meanest, toughest little girl I've ever met." Or he'd corner Jeff on the porch outside and in a loud stage whisper say, "Your wife is so scary." The ultimate compliment.

That day we passed the Ed Hackett inspection. It's a good thing, too, since he's basically the unofficial mayor around here. He's been in this community his whole life, so when he invited Jeff to drink whiskey by the woodstove with the guys on Sundays (sorry Hil, no chicks allowed), we knew we'd earned our stripes.

Our good fortune was snowballing. We'd been farmers for just a few short months, and Jeff got offered dream jobs, back to back. The only catch was that they were in Mexico. The first was a no-brainer. Alfonso and Jonás Cuarón, fresh off the success of *Gravity*, wanted him to play the bad guy versus Gael García Bernal in a story about the Texas-Mexico border, *Desierto*. It was a great script. The moment Jeff said yes, his next bucket-list job presented itself—the miniseries *Texas Rising*. This project would also shoot in Mexico, and not in coastal resort—jeweled Mexico either, so it wouldn't be easy to travel back and forth, and cell phone coverage would be spotty. They were shooting in Durango, a little town where there had recently been a series of beheadings related to drug trafficking. When I googled "Durango," a big red State Department alert popped up, which basically said that Americans shouldn't go there and federal employees couldn't go there.

I never told Jeff not to do it. I knew it was his dream job, and if he didn't go, it would be four months of moaning about not doing it.

But I still struggled with how he had to leave so quickly, especially to a place that was so dangerous. There was even some fear about danger on set. He'd be riding a horse for the role, and before he left, he was adamant about making sure there was a good trainer and the horse was healthy and comfortable being on the set. But once he got down there, he found that his horse was just a baby and wasn't broken at all. Jeff is an animal whisperer and all, but they had cannons going off and were filming huge raid scenes at full gallop with guns a-firing. In my mind, every day on that bucking horse meant possible impending death.

Meanwhile, back at the farm, I had a bathtub full of birds, and was just trying not to get electrocuted.

9

My candle burns at both ends;
It will not last the night;
But ah, my foes, and oh, my friends—
It gives a lovely light!

**—Edna St. Vincent Millay,
"Figs from Thistles: First Fig"**

We had record snows that first winter at Mischief Farm, which meant that when April came around and the sun was out, swift creeks were flowing all over the property. It was perfect territory for a wild little boy. One day, I was up to my eyeballs in the wallpaper I was taking down in the old farmhouse when Gus called me out to play in the creek. Bisou pranced down the driveway to join us, stopping to stare down and reluctantly touch noses with the alpacas. Bisou was the grand dame of the farm and made sure every creature knew it. I showed Gus how to make little boats out of leaves, and we discarded our shoes and soaked our feet in the snow-cold water till they were numb. We lay in the neon green first grass of the season, Gus in the crook of my arm, the sun warm on our faces, Bisou rolling in the grass beside us.

I was blissfully happy, but even so, I could feel tears spring to my eyes. *Jeff would love this*, I thought. *Where was he right now? Was he safe?* We'd bought this farm together, and he was missing this glorious first spring. We had everything we ever wanted, and yet we were apart.

To keep myself from missing Jeff too much, I filled the days with busy work. Dozens of half barrels with questionable plantings in them were on the property, and I was determined to make each one a ruckus of color. Every day on my way to drop Gus at school I'd see a "U-Cut" flower farm. *Hell, I can do that!*, I thought. There was a large, unsightly mess of mud outside the big barn where the thoroughbred horse manure pile had been. Could I have planted grass and let it gradually fill in? Sure. But that would have been boring. Instead, I piled up rocks from all over the property, built a minor retaining wall around the irregular shape, and overturned the earth, making rows of sunflowers and zinnias and bachelor buttons and snapdragons. Sunny had left behind a lone raised bed. It was ten feet wide and thirty feet long and just enough space to give vegetables the old college try. To the left I put in trellises to catch snow peas as they climbed. In front I popped in bush green beans, hoping Gus would take to them the way my little brother John had as a kid. To split the garden in half longways, I put in a row of carrots and beets. The middle of the garden was home to yellow squash and zucchini (which really *do* need all the space that's called for on the back of the seed packet!), and the right side of the garden was tomato city. My mother always said, "Don't grow anything you can find in the grocery store." I heeded that and was lucky enough to find the local Hudson Valley Seed Company, which promoted heritage versions of native plants. Purple carrots? Yes, please. If Jeff was going to risk life and limb, the least I could do was ensure that the home he returned to was a fairy tale.

It was hard work, and it took a toll on me. I would take Gus to school in the morning and do manual labor on the farm all day, so Gus was lucky if I didn't show up smelling of poop, with clumps of fur and feathers sticking to various parts of my anatomy.

One day, running late to pick up Gus from school, I slicked my hair back into an Evita-bun and threw on Jeff's Carhartt pants, his flannel shirt, a jacket, and boots. I pulled into the school parking lot and noticed that one of the other mothers, whom I'd known for more than a year, was craning her neck to get a good look at me. I looked over my shoulder, but no one else was there. As I got closer, she looked at me with a horrified expression.

"Hey, what's going on?" I asked.

She blushed. "Hilarie! I'm so sorry. I thought you were a cute new dad."

At least she thought I was cute.

Any vanity I'd once had was now diverted to the farm. Why color my hair roots when I could spend that time planting outrageous bursts of catmint? The money I once would have put into vintage clothes or the obligatory Los Angeles pedicure went into hydrangea bushes and gallons and gallons of paint. The upside was, I had never been in better shape. I spent my days shoveling, lugging, and digging. Manual labor on the farm was the new SoulCycle.

It was worth it. I became giddy as I looked at the splendor of the multitudes of awakening bulbs—crocuses, daffodils, hyacinths, tulips. The typical mature bulb can multiply itself by twenty every five years, so an entire history of floral fortitude showed off in the yard.

My Magic Potion

From the age of three until, well . . . now, Gus has told his peers, doctors, teachers, and anyone else who will listen that his mother is a witch. It began with a "monsters in the closet" situation, where I cast a protection spell on his bedroom and assured him I could hex anything. Including my age. Young Gus believed that the blood-red liquid in my glass each evening was a supernatural elixir meant to disguise my true age of 108 and keep me young forever. Close. It was really a mixture of raw apple cider vinegar, lemon juice, and beet juice.

Coming off of *One Tree Hill*, my whole body was toxic. I'd had a hell of a good time getting into such bad shape. But if I was gonna be a back-to-nature earth mama, I needed some natural support to get back on track. Hence, my potion.

First, the lemon juice. Lemon has been credited with relieving stress and energizing your body, while lowering blood pressure, flushing out toxins, reducing the production of free radicals, which age you, and keeping your teeth and mouth healthy. Beet juice helps me with my low iron. (Ladies, ever feel like your hair is thinning at the temples? I did after childbirth. Low iron is the culprit!) Headaches? Shortness of breath? Dizziness? I used to think in my late teens and early twenties that I was having anxiety attacks. Nope. Iron again. Beets have all the earthy goodness that we need to recoup after a hard day and replenish energy. They are a magical root that grounds your body.

And then there's the most important ingredient, apple cider vinegar. I could go on and on about the advantages of ACV, which has been used for thousands of years as a cure-all. But for me, its most important job was fixing my skin. I had horrible, embarrassing acne for years. Dermatologists threw all manner of chemicals at me, but nothing worked. In the end, I realized that my body's pH was off—probably from eating too much sugar. Consuming ACV reset that. And facials made of ACV, local honey, and a touch of lemon did wonders to clear my skin and lighten up any dark scars.

Hilarie's Magic Potion

8 ounces apple cider vinegar
8 ounces beet juice
4 ounces lemon juice
Water

In a large jar or pitcher, mix together apple cider vinegar, beet juice, and lemon juice. (I keep this in the fridge, and it lasts a little longer than a week.) Each night, fill a glass half full of the mixture and then dilute it with cold water to fill the glass.

It takes a minute to acclimate to the taste, since it's puckery and earthy. But as I explained to Gus, it's magic, a potion that contains the elements of nature. Water. The beet represents earth. The lemon is light and bright like the air. And the apple cider vinegar burns like fire.

Even with all the blood, sweat, and tears, I felt like I was coming back to the truest version of myself. The Hilarie before MTV or TV shows. Before self-consciousness had entered my orbit. I was Virginia Hilarie again. Planting bulbs and seeds, working with manure, reminded me of a time when I was eight years old, and a pickup truck of horse manure was delivered to our house along with a miniature horse. (Not a pony, mind you. Don't you dare make that mistake.) Although my brothers and I were mildly interested in the not-pony, we were more interested in the manure. It was standard practice for us Burton kids to get really dirty in the backyard and for my parents to just turn the hose on us. (You can't bathe four kids in a bathtub at the same time.) No one else in the neighborhood had a huge pile of poop in their yard. It was exotic. And I knew all the other kids were looking over the fence thinking, *What fun is going on in the Burton house?*

Raking manure across my garden bed also made me think a lot about my mother and *her* garden, which had started as an act of self-preservation. She was nineteen when she met my father and not much older when they were married. Having no money, but a big imagination, flowers became her way of expressing herself. My mother could grow roses bigger than my head, and as a young child, I thought she must have had some kind of magic.

After a few years and three more kids, we moved to a two-story house on the south side of town. As a kid, I had no idea how dire our financial situation was. We had *stairs* and a laundry room and a big flat backyard! We were rich! I thought. But looking back, I can see my mother moving in, clocking the chipped-up linoleum floor and the marigold-colored appliances, the ripped-up wallpaper and the endless projects ahead of her and my dad. "I will plant a garden," she must have said, surveying that vast yard of dirt patches and crabgrass.

She started off with a little strawberry patch and then expanded. She had corn, beans, tomatoes, cucumbers—and she grew flowers: daylilies, all her Dutch-heritage bulbs, and black-eyed Susans. The garden was an epicenter of activity. Even when we were inside, life was infused by the garden. We were a windows-wide-open family. The scent of cut grass, tomatoes, dirt, and vinegar—those were the smells of my childhood, and I was so happy to be giving that to Gus. When he wasn't in school, he was out in the dirt with me.

One summer my brothers and I discovered that you can eat daylilies. Tentatively at first, Billy and I split a petal and nibbled at its edges. As the older kids, it was our job to risk our lives in the name of science. "It's *good*!" we informed the others. We ate flowers like we were gobbling up sunshine.

"What have you done?" my poor mother cried. She didn't have to worry about deer or wildlife chewing her flowers; it was her children. Guilt still tastes like orange lilies to me.

Later that April, I was in our bedroom, hanging new curtains and lamenting that I wasn't outside, when my phone buzzed. It was a text from Janice, who owned the antique shop in Rhinebeck next to Samuel's.

Honey, call me.

That was odd. Anyone who knows me understands that I don't like to talk on the phone. So something must have been wrong.

I looked out over the pastures as the phone rang.

"Hello," Janice answered. Her voice was thick with tears.

"Oh no, what's wrong?"

"Ira is gone."

Everything else she said became a blur of noise far away. My brain became gauze. Questions lodged, then disappeared.

Ira, who was always so fiercely alive, had been sick. Ira, who had been our guardian angel, had been working too hard. Ira, who was only ten years older than Jeff and was active and healthy, had collapsed.

Ira, who was good and generous and had a heart of gold, also had a heart that quit.

"I just know how close you guys were with him," Janice said. "I didn't want you to hear it through the rumor mill."

I dropped to the floor in the middle of the room. "Thank you for telling me."

After we hung up, I wanted to talk to Jeff, to tell him myself, but he was out of cell range in Durango so I texted him.

Babe, I really need you to call me when you get a free moment.

Bisou ambled over and put her head in my lap. I ran my fingers through her thick fur and inhaled dog and earth and farm. I was still holding my phone and realized I wanted to talk someone. I was itching to do something, to help. I wanted community. But what I really wanted was to drive into town and sit with Ira.

One by one, everyone from town started sending me messages. Gus's teacher, shop owners, parents from school: We know Ira was your friend . . . Ira loved you and Jeff . . . Did you hear the news about Ira?

I texted Jules, then Phoebe and Andy, and they all asked me how they could help.

When I picked Gus up from school, there was a parade of somber glances. I put on a brave face for my boy and spent the night doting on him. He fell asleep in my room watching a movie, his little head buried in my shoulder. My phone lit up on my nightstand.

It was Jeffrey. It was late. He had been in the desert all day doing dangerous stunts. We were thousands of miles apart, and words were not the balm either of us needed. He isn't someone who wants to talk when he's upset. He just wanted to get home.

"Will you go to the funeral?"

"Of course."

"And find John Traver. Tell him not to close the shop. Tell him we will take care of it."

"Okay."

"Tell him anything that he needs, just let us know."

"Okay, honey, I'll tell him." I was saying okay, but I was thinking, *What are you talking about? Close the shop?*

The next day, the bench in front of Samuel's had become a shrine to Ira. Flowers and cards and stuffed animals were piled high, including a few of those beloved Sinterklaas teddy bears. A huge crowd had gathered in the shop. John Traver was juggling the tasks of comforting the bereaved and still serving coffee and sweets to the endless procession of locals. I gave John a wave across the room. "You okay?" He nodded bravely. Helping him was a high school kid, Vincent. These two young men were now tasked with holding up an entire town of Ira's bereaved friends.

The service was two days later. "I'm gonna get a sitter and go if anyone is interested," I emailed Andy and Phoebe and the Rudds. Our emails spun into long, sentimental, and funny threads, and with Jeff off filming, it was good to be connected to close friends. It felt foreign to take off my farm clothes and put on a skirt and grownup shoes. The funeral home was down the street from the candy store, and when I got there the entire Rhinebeck community wrapped around the block, waiting to get in.

I saw Barbara and Dick. They had opened up their department store around the same time as Ira had opened Samuel's, so they had been with him since day one. Pam and Roger Hoffman saw that I was alone and took me under their wings. Ira's family had traveled in from Westchester. His husband was in the front row. The whole town filled the funeral home. Ira was everyone's adopted family member; we all considered him an uncle or brother or son— something closer, more integral than our friend.

The place was bursting with flowers, grief, and love. Ira's husband said that they'd been planning a big wedding celebration since their real wedding had been so small, and his eulogy included the vows they had recited to each other. Then he played "their" song, Roberta Flack's version of "The First Time Ever I Saw Your Face," and I thought I'd crack open right there.

After the service Roger and Pam and I went to find John Traver. He was with his wife, Ally, his high school sweetheart, and he looked a little cowed by the whole thing.

I touched his arm. "How are you doing?"

"It's been awful. The store has been a weeklong wake that I've been hosting. It's been hard to be there." John was being so honest, but I could also see him choosing his words carefully. "I don't

know what I'm going to do. I hope I don't have to close the store."
I still wasn't sure exactly what he meant, but I understood that the
words were code for *shit has hit the fan*. John was rattled. All eyes
were on him. Every single person in town was asking, "What are
you going to do?" And he didn't have an answer.

"Listen John," I told him. "I spoke with Jeff, and we are here to
help you with whatever you need. Just don't close the shop."

Burton Pickle Recipes

Mom's pickles were a big deal. Our kitchen was always stocked with her mustard seeds, her dill, her sugar (depending on whether we were making sweet pickles or sour pickles), and a lot of vinegar. The pickles were one of the ways I could tell my parents really loved each other. It was chaos at our house during the day, but when Dad came home from work and saw Mom's pickles on the table, his favorite, he would get that "I love you" look in his eye. You don't have to say "I love you" when you're acting it out. My parents don't exchange cards and gifts, but they've always done meaningful things for each other to express their love.

Of course I make pickles too. Gus is a pickle nut. He has to have them in his lunch box every single day. Jeffrey and Gus love everything really spicy so I began growing jalapeños and cucumbers in the garden to make sweet, hot pickles. My mom always wanted me to hold on to my Iowa roots, so she and I spent a lot of time together pickling and canning. I joke with my mother about writing a cookbook called *Piss and Vinegar.* These two recipes would definitely be included.

Fresh-Packed Dill Pickles

Making a fresh-packed pickle keeps the cucumbers crunchy, rather than soft and cooked when they are canned. That said, they don't last as long either, so I make them in smaller batches.

18 to 20 pickling cucumbers (3 to 3½ inches long)

3¾ cups water

2½ cups vinegar (5% to 6% acidity) (I use white vinegar, and Mom uses apple
cider vinegar)

¼ cup + 1 tablespoon pickling or noniodized salt

3 heads fresh dill

3 slices onion, ½ inch thick

3 cloves garlic

1 tsp mustard seeds

Peppercorns, to taste

Optional: Jalapeño, sliced into ¼ inch pieces (if you want a kick!)

3 sterilized quart jars (dunk 'em in boiling water)

Wash cucumbers. Mix water, vinegar, and salt in a Dutch oven; bring to
a boil. Add a head of dill, a clove of garlic, and an onion slice to each
of three hot quart jars. Sprinkle the mustard seeds evenly amongst
the jars and add jalapeños if desired. Keep in mind, the more jalapeño
seeds you put in, the hotter your pickles will be! Pack cucumbers
in jars, leaving ½ inch headspace. Cover with brine, leaving ½ inch
headspace. Let cucumbers and pickling juice cool completely before
screwing on lids and refrigerating.

Store in the fridge.

Quick Pickles

My dad really likes quick pickles. He likes them sweet, so my mom
uses rice wine vinegar instead of apple cider vinegar and sugar instead
of salt.

18 to 20 pickling cucumbers (3 to 3½ inches long), cut into round slices ¼ inch thick

3¾ cups water

2½ cups rice wine vinegar

(continued)

¼ cup + 1 tablespoon sugar
3 slices onion, ½ inch thick
Mustard seeds, to taste
Peppercorns, to taste
Salt
Optional: Chili flakes or chili pepper

Wash cucumbers. Mix water, vinegar, and sugar; toss in onions, mustard seeds, peppercorns, and a pinch of salt. I add chili flakes or some sort of chili pepper to the quick pickles. (We make everything sweet-hot.) Everything should be to your taste; that's the beauty of making things at home.

You don't need to cook the brine. Instead, pack cucumbers in jars, pour the brine over the cucumbers, screw on lids, and set the jars in the fridge. They'll be ready to eat in a couple of hours; they're even better the next day!

Store in the fridge.

And honey, you can pickle anything you pull out of the garden—carrots, green beans, onions, watermelon rinds. Get creative! Hell, pickled tomatoes are better than any ketchup.

Part Three

HARVEST

10

I am beginning to learn that it is the sweet, simple
things of life which are the real ones after all.

—Laura Ingalls Wilder, "A Bouquet of Wild Flowers"

I'm not sure how seriously John took me at the funeral when
I told him Jeff and I were ready to help with the shop. The
month of April dragged on, and John exhausted himself
working six days a week, opening the shop early and then staying hours after closing to try to right the ship.

One day in the store, I leaned on the counter. "Jeff is busting his
butt to get home, buddy. He wants to help. What's going on here?"

It turned out the answer was debt. It was 2014, and the economy had been in a free fall for enough years that stores which sold
frivolous things like coffee and candy had taken a hit. Bills were
months past due. Various suppliers and merchants had done lots
of favors for Ira, because he was such a great guy. Favors had accu-
mulated, and now they were looming over John.

"I really want to keep the shop open for the twentieth reunion
later this month," he told me. "That was Ira's goal. You want to see
something?" John pulled a worn photo album from the tiny back
office. Handing it over to me, he explained, "It's the opening day
party. Look how young everyone is."

I flipped through the glossy cellophane pages. There were Barb and Dick, grinning with their plastic cups of wine. Celeste, the shop's chocolate maker, in a cute nineties sundress. Faces I recognized from the shop smiled or stuck out a tongue, hamming it up. And there was Ira, with his thick curly hair, not a trace of gray, wearing a suit and beaming. His dream sprawled across the pages of that album.

John eased himself into the chair beside me. It was as if all the panic and adrenaline that had fueled his long days since Ira had passed just drained away. He rubbed the heels of his hands into his eyes.

In a quiet voice John told me about how his birth father had died the day after he was born. He was lucky though, because not only did he have this wonderful stepfather, Roger Hoffman, but he had also had Ira, who hadn't had any children of his own. All through high school John had been Ira's star employee, and after John got a business degree at college, Ira created a second manager position for him and paid John's salary out of his own pocket just to keep him at the store.

"He used to joke all the time, 'John I'm going to leave the shop to you.'" John gave me a wry smile and my stomach pitched, overwhelmed by the thought of all the debt Samuel's had racked up and that Ira's dream was in danger.

A couple of weeks later, Jeffrey made a short trip home. We invited Andy, Phoebe, Paul, and Julie out for Saturday night sushi at Osaka. Usually, Jeff was obsessed with appetizers and always ordered far too many, completely stuffing himself before dinner arrived, but that night he was focused. As we were all sitting down at the table, Jeff launched his idea: "I think we should buy the candy store."

Surprised, I turned my head and looked at him, silently asking, *What are you talking about?* We had talked about helping John, but now we were buying a candy store?

If the others were surprised too, it didn't last long. In fact, it wasn't even a discussion; everyone was on board. We loved Ira, and Samuel's was an institution in our town. We could not let it turn into an anonymous franchise store. This was not a business opportunity for us; this was a save-Samuel's-for-the-town situation. It was a preservation initiative.

John Traver agreed to meet with us, so we three couples with four children in tow gathered at Samuel's, the eleven of us crowded around two tiny tables as John laid out the worst-case scenario for the shop—how much monthly overhead was, how much money was owed to various vendors. He paused as he spoke, careful with his words.

It was pretty dire. Samuel's was deeply in debt. Then, John quietly admitted that he hadn't cashed a paycheck in two months because there wasn't enough money in the account. He showed us the equipment. A huge refrigerator took up half the shop and didn't work; the coffee machines needed attention, and the coffee wasn't great. Ira had started ordering the cheapest supplies he could get; the candy was all penny candy. Everything was an economy choice, yet still the shop had maintained its charm because of Ira.

John knew it was going to be daunting to step into the shoes Ira

Rhubarb Preserves

Rhubarb takes a couple of seasons to come in; you have to plant it and let it grow for two years. So while I still had to earn my gardening stripes at Mischief Farm, I pillaged the farmers' market for the best rhubarb, with its bright pink and red stalks. My great-grandfather, Dirk Kolenbrander, used to make a strawberry-rhubarb preserve that he would send through relatives to us, all the way from Iowa, where he was a reverend. He was a regal-looking man, with snow-white hair and vintage browline glasses that were so old they became hip again. He wore inexpensive but beautiful suits and raised bright children with my great-grandma Nellie.

The image of this elegant man rolling up his sleeves and making preserves in between writing sermons always captivated me. The preserves would arrive in recycled plastic containers, and us kids would crowd around the table, where mom would slather hunks of bread with Great-Grandpa-Dirk-strawberry-rhubarb preserves and dole them out. Then Mom added rhubarb to the strawberries in her garden so she could make it too. Now I use that recipe to make my own preserves.

I'm a preservationist, and Jeffrey is too. In a way, moving to Rhinebeck was an act of preservation. Both self-preservation and also the preservation of a set of ideals—volunteerism and community.

After watching the mom-and-pop shops of our childhoods get swallowed up by big box stores and strip malls, we'd found a new, safe place in Rhinebeck. Losing Ira was hard, and the idea of losing

Samuel's was devastating, given the twenty years of love Ira had put in to the store, giving all of us in town a place we considered "our spot."

Ira had planted the shop. We were gonna keep making the jam.

Kolenbrander Strawberry-Rhubarb Jam

2 cups fresh strawberries, crushed
4 cups chopped fresh rhubarb
¼ cup bottled lemon juice
1 package (1¾ ounces) powdered fruit pectin
5½ cups sugar

In a Dutch oven, combine strawberries, rhubarb, and lemon juice. Stir in pectin. Bring to a full rolling boil, stirring constantly. Stir in sugar. Return to a full rolling boil. Boil and stir for 1 minute. Remove from heat. Skim off foam. Ladle hot mixture into six hot, sterilized pint jars, leaving ¼ inch headspace. Remove air bubbles and adjust headspace if necessary by adding hot mixture. Wipe rims. Center lids of jars. Screw on bands until fingertip tight.

Place jars into canner with simmering water, ensuring they are completely covered with water. Bring to a boil. Process for 5 minutes. Remove jars and cool.

left behind. He was shy. He was very thoughtful. He remembered every customer's name down to every kid who came into the shop. But, being a dynamic force like Ira is a lot day in and day out. It would require a big change of personality and extroverted energy, and we needed to know whether John really wanted that. Our other fear was that we were going to buy the place and then John, the person who held all the knowledge and all the relationships with the vendors, who was the key to the whole business, would decide to leave. He had already been offered a significantly higher-paying job at the Wells Fargo bank in town.

I knew it was his life and his decision to make. I asked him point blank: "John, what do you want out of your life? Do you what to be the town candy man until you retire, or is this just a chapter for you?"

The town is in John's blood. His father had been a beloved member of the town council. Streets are named after his family, which goes back to the 1700s. And his parents are small business owners here in the community. So I wasn't surprised when he said without hesitation, "I want to do this forever."

We were so relieved. John was the key to making sure that this was going to work.

As we started gathering the kids, John put his hand over his heart and said, "You don't know what this means to me."

Next, we went to Ira's husband and asked whether he would be interested in selling the business to us. We offered to buy it for the amount of debt that the shop owed so he could pay off all the debt and clear Ira's name.

Grief is a confusing thing, and everyone grieves differently. Given the shop's debt, Ira's husband seemed to see-saw between being happy that we were trying to save the shop and resentful that Samuel's existed at all. The negotiations lasted from May to December, but during that time, the friendships among our group of friends were fortified, along with our resolve to make sure Samuel's thrived.

Meanwhile, other people were circling the shop, coming in the doors with real estate agents. One investor wanted to turn it into a cybercafé, and another person wanted to turn it into a bicycle shop. All of a sudden, people who had not been friends with John Traver were showing up asking a lot of questions.

The building was owned by a gentleman who owned a number of places in the historic district and lived in Florida. The landlord, Joan, ran everything for him in town, and her son Bill was the building manager of the shop; so I went out to lunch with Joan and learned everything I could—that they hadn't been charging Ira what they could have for rent, and that they hadn't raised the rent in years because they knew he couldn't afford it. Joan was gun-shy about asking us for more, but we knew that there were things that needed to be fixed that Ira hadn't mentioned to them because he was so ashamed that he wasn't paying the rent. The bathroom had a leak, the floor needed to be fixed, the place had electrical issues and a number of outlets that didn't work, and the back screen door was falling off and needed paint. During the months that we were negotiating with Ira's husband, we were also getting our ducks in a row.

We decided that Andy, Julie, and I would be the managing partners and that we would report back to Phoebe, Paul, and Jeff. Andy and I would take our kids with us when we met with the accountant who had been doing Ira's taxes. We saw this as an opportunity to teach our kids about business so when they grew up they'd have no issue going into the office of an accountant or a lawyer. We took them to our lawyer meetings with John Marvin. We took them to the bank branch in Rhinebeck when we opened our new account with David Tellerday—yes, he's a banker and his name is Tellerday. He let the kids play with the stuff on his desk while we figured out what type of account to open.

The town rallied around the preservation of Samuel's. Everybody wanted the business to succeed. It was Ira's legacy, and a Rhinebeck institution.

Friends and neighbors in the community doubled down. David began coming in regularly for coffee and maybe a sweet or two. He observed the way things had been done for years and made helpful suggestions. "Open earlier!" he urged us. "Get the crowd coming in before work." Dick and Barb would pop over from the department store to see how everything was evolving and to pat John and me on the back. "Keep going," they said. Parents from Gus's school became more and more visible in the shop, bringing the kids in after class. This wasn't just lip service. The community showed up. And they kept showing up.

People who hire all these things done for them
never know what they lose; for the homeliest
tasks get beautified if loving hands do them.

—**Louisa May Alcott**, *Little Women*

A month and a half passed as we worked hard to negotiate and navigate the details to buy Samuel's. During that time, Jeff was still down in Durango shooting the movie, and when he assured me that things were not nearly as dangerous as the interweb made it seem, Gus and I ventured down.

Durango looks like a town out of a Western movie, complete with a baroque cathedral and an old town prison that has been converted into a hotel, which is where the cast was staying. The tiny rooms used to be jail cells, and there were no better cellmates than my boys. Plus, Chad Michael Murray, my character Peyton's husband from *One Tree Hill*, was staying right next door to Jeffrey. My two "husbands," neither of them legal! Besides Chad, Jeff was working with a fun pack of guys that included Ray Liotta, Chris McDonald, and Bill Paxton, who became Jeff's closest friend on the project.

The prison yard was now a courtyard with a pool that sat dead center in the hotel, with all of the cellblocks overlooking it. All the dudes hung out there when they weren't filming. Bill would bring down his huge hardback copy of his character Sam Houston's biography and excitedly spout off fun facts about the legend. Bill loved his work. His energy was contagious. Gus called him Uncle Bill and reveled in the attention of these rough and rowdy guys.

One day by the pool, the guys were raving about Gus, and out of nowhere, Jeff announced in front of all of them that we were trying to have another kid. We'd been busy with settling into Mischief Farm and buying Samuel's so hadn't talked further about having another baby. It was news to me that he was on board, but I'd take that news any way I could get it!

Bill was also on board with this plan and cried out, "All right man! We'll watch Gus. Go make it happen now!" It was mildly mortifying.

Gus and I returned home, and Samuel's stayed open by the skin of its teeth. By August it seemed like the deal was going to go through, and come hell or high water I was going to make it work. I lived by the philosophy that if you act like something's going to go wrong, it will go wrong. If, however, you act like it's going to go right, it will go right. I could hear my dad's voice saying the "want-to" creates the "how-to."

I took it as a sign when I woke up to a text from our groundskeeper Awesome early one morning.

There's more cows.

Now ol' Ed Hackett and I had become quite fond of each other by that point. When you get past the rough exterior, you realize Ed is just a guy who really loves his wife, Barb, and their kids and cares a heck of a lot about his community. When he saw how much money we were wasting on tractor gas to mow all our fields, he said, "Why don't you dummies just let me put some cows in those fields? They'll handle your grass." Genius. We've been boarding his dairy cows ever since. So when Awesome said there were more cows, I just thought Ed or his son Ed Junior had gotten a jump on the day and dropped more cows off at the crack of dawn.

I texted Awesome back.

Okay, great.

Quickly he responded.

BABY!

Baby?! We had a pregnant cow? Still in my pajamas, I threw on boots and raced down to the front pasture in the Rhino. Sure enough, the big chubby cow I thought had just been super lazy in the August heat was not so chubby anymore and was standing guard over her five-minute-old baby. Baby cow hadn't even stood up yet. He was still covered in gunk and his mama licked at him, loving him through the grooming. Gus was still asleep. Jeff was a world away. I'd been so lonely and unsure of things with the store, then this miracle happened on *our* farm and the whole world was right again.

I've always believed in signs from the universe. I was a kid who prayed for signs. I would walk to and from school, talking to myself and noticing odd occurrences and taking them as motivation. The flowers are up early—things are going to be great today. There's a dead baby bird on the ground by the holly bush—I'm done for.

Privately, I was hoping the calf's birth was a sign that I'd get pregnant again soon. Although with Jeff away and me ensconced in Samuel's, it would have taken a whole lot more than a mere sign—it would have taken a goddamn miracle to conceive on the few days we were actually in the same place.

When Gus started school again in September, I created a new routine: drop kiddo off, head over to Samuel's, do as much as I could to spruce up the place without making it seem like I was doing anything, as we hadn't legally taken ownership yet, pick up kiddo, head back to farm, hurry out to garden to harvest our first crop of veggies, do rounds on the animals, collect eggs, feed child and dogs, bathe child, bedtime. And then after Gus fell asleep, I'd try to cram in all the paperwork and emails I'd ignored all day.

Whenever we took ownership of Samuel's, I wanted the shop to be in good order and a reflection of the love and effort we were all putting into it. To get there, the shop needed a cleaning. A *thorough* cleaning. John was fanatical about the merchandise and making sure the shelves were dusted and arranged in a tidy fashion. But endless boxes were piled up, the ceiling leaked, the bathroom was in shambles, and there was a trashcan that hadn't been moved in years. I started pulling everything out from its settled place and uncovered an avalanche of housekeeping. It was like stumbling into a fifteen-year-old boy's room and opening the closet door to find all the hidden dirty laundry. Essentially, what Samuel's needed was a mother. I brought cleaning supplies, snapped on a pair of rubber gloves, and got to work.

The rumor mill in Rhinebeck didn't have to work very hard before word spread that a bunch of actors were buying the shop, and one of them was literally on her hands and knees scrubbing the shop from top to bottom. Locals started popping in just to see the spectacle of the teen-drama actress turned janitor. Some people had been grumbling about how these "city people" were going to come in and ruin what had been a good thing. And I get it. Ira was beloved, and the shop truly was a small-town treasure. I understand why people would be concerned about "outsiders" (and Hollywood outsiders, at that!) coming in and turning it into something else. Once we started sprucing the place up, however, John confided in me that people had commented on it to him, saying how they were changing their minds about the upcoming new ownership.

Once the cleaning mission was complete, one particular eyesore gnawed at me until I couldn't take it anymore. All along the entire counter of the shop, plates of enticing baked goods were lined up. It would have been a feast for the eyes if not for the scratched-up and yellowing two-by-four-foot sheet of Plexiglas that was supposed to keep germy hands and faces away. It was the least enticing baked goods display on the planet.

We didn't own the place yet; negotiations were dragging on and on. But if Samuel's was ever going to be the cute boutique sweet shop it was destined to be, we had to get rid of that enormous sneeze guard.

Zucchini for the Win

Sometimes you just really need a win, an easy layup, a sure thing. During that first year at Mischief Farm, when I was desperately searching for signs that we'd made the right choice and everything was going to be okay, little things could make or break me. Success in the garden was the best of the best signs. And the zucchini in particular were glorious for my ego.

Honestly, it's a pretty easy plant. The seeds are big and easy to manage. The plants aren't fussy about water. And once you get them going, they churn out an absurd amount of food. The blossoms are the loveliest of delicacies, and by now we've all seen zucchini ribbons served as pasta, or baked with parmesan cheese, or turned into addictive zucchini bread. Zucchini is a gem with many talents.

I wanted to find a way to use the abundance of eggs our hens were laying with the heaping baskets of zucchini we gathered multiple times a week. Hence, this Mischief Farm take on the classic Eggs Benedict.

Zucchini Fritter Benedict (Vegetarian)

FOR THE FRITTERS

1 pound zucchini (about 2 medium/large around 12 inches long)

1 teaspoon + ½ teaspoon kosher or sea salt

2 eggs, beaten

Zest of one lemon

1 tablespoon fresh thyme

¼ cup chopped scallion

½ cup all-purpose flour

½ teaspoon baking powder

¼ teaspoon black pepper

Canola oil for pan

FOR THE SAUCE

½ cup crème fraîche

1½ tablespoons lemon juice

1 teaspoon Dijon mustard

1 tablespoon mayonnaise

1 teaspoon hot sauce

1 teaspoon lemon zest

Paprika

3 chives, chopped

FOR THE POACHED EGGS

4 fresh eggs

Rice vinegar

Salt

Trim ends of zucchini. Grate and place in fine-mesh colander; mix with 1 teaspoon salt and let sit for 10 minutes with colander draining over a bowl.

Meanwhile, make sauce. Mix crème fraîche with lemon juice, mustard, mayo, and hot sauce. Stir in zest and chives.

(continued)

Squeeze out remaining liquid from zucchini using a clean dish towel. You should have around 2 cups of zucchini. Place in a mixing bowl and add beaten eggs, lemon zest, thyme, and scallion.

In a small bowl combine ½ teaspoon salt, flour, baking powder, and black pepper. Sprinkle over the zucchini mixture and combine.

Heat 2 tablespoons canola oil in a nonstick skillet over medium high heat.

Add 2-tablespoon scoops of batter into the pan and flatten with a spatula. Cook until golden brown, about 2 minutes; then flip and cook the other side until golden brown. Place in warming drawer or oven set at a low temperature.

To poach the eggs, boil water in a saucepan and then reduce to a simmer. Add rice vinegar and salt to water.

Crack eggs into a cup one at a time. Create a vortex with a whisk in the water and slip eggs, one at a time, into hot water. Cook for 4 minutes. Remove egg and let dry on paper towel.

Place a fritter on a plate and put a poached egg on top. Drizzle with sauce and sprinkle lightly with paprika and chopped chives.

ENJOY!!

I went over to HomeGoods across the Hudson River and bought every cake stand with a glass dome that they had. When we set them up in all their varying heights and colors, the salad bar vibe was gone, and our baked goods sparkled like gems in playful jewel boxes.

"Ira would have liked this," John said. It made me sad to think about all the awesome things Ira would have done if he'd only had the capital. He had such a big imagination.

By the time October rolled around, Jeff was home again for a short visit and amazed by all the hard work we'd put in around the farm and the shop. All of the buildings on our property had been transformed with paint; our plantings had reached maturity; the sunflowers were ten feet tall; the garden was a machine of productivity; and the chickens were laying eggs at such a rate I couldn't give them away fast enough. John Traver became my dealer of sorts. I'd keep him flush with eggs, and then he'd dole out extras to our bakers and friends who had done favors for the shop. On other occasions, I'd take a big shopping bag of egg crates to the preschool parking lot and thank the parents for supporting Samuel's. In my experience, bottles of wine and fresh eggs are the two gifts people get most excited about.

Then, on top of everything, I decided on a whim to renovate the farm kitchen in the wee hours of the morning after I'd put Gus to sleep. I knew it was gonna be a while before we had time to fully renovate it, and with the garden going nuts as it was, I was spending a significant amount of time in that space. But I needed the kitchen to be bright and airy and tidy. Over the course of a week, I covered the dark green tile on the countertops and backsplash with a concrete kit. Lemme tell you something: concrete makes everything cooler. I was meticulous about sanding between each layer of concrete to get a smooth, polished finish. Once that was done, I sanded down the cabinets and painted them a bright, soft white. The kitchen immediately seemed bigger. I also planned a special touch for Jeffrey. Remember how much he loves red? I threw him a bone and painted the kitchen island red. It was, of course, the first thing he noticed when he got home, and as I had hoped, he loved it.

We spent Halloween together, going pumpkin picking with Andy, Phoebe, and the Rudds. The kids ran hay mazes together, and we all oohed over the donkeys and goats. But then Jeff was off again: "It's a fun script; Robert De Niro is producing and acting in it." I didn't want him to leave again, but who am I to deny a man his opportunity to work with De Niro?

Jeff made it back just in time for Thanksgiving, which we spent with the Rudds again. Julie and Paul's excitement about things is intoxicating, and while the kids wrestled and chased each other, we conspired over Samuel's. We planned to get as many local artisans as we could, and someone mentioned checking out the chocolate festival across the river. We had fun dreaming of all we could do with the shop.

The day after Thanksgiving John and I created the Christmas display for the shop window. Ira had loved creating scenes and dioramas for that window. John showed me another photo album. "Check this out," he said, flipping to a shot of the window, complete with an antique fireplace mantel, stockings, fake snow, and a slew of presents. It was exactly the kind of display that begged you to come on in.

A bar table ran the length of the window now, so doing anything quite that elaborate was out of the question. But if I could just make something colorful and shallow, we could slip it in between the table and glass. Much to Jeffrey's dismay, this sent me into turbo craft mode. He'd worked so hard to get home, and there I was hiding out in the basement with a glue gun, some foam core, a razor knife, paints, and an array of gorgeous handmade paper I picked up from our new pal Doug at the Rhinebeck Artist's Shop in town.

As we counted down the days until our ownership of the shop would become official, and also Christmas, I made an Advent calendar for the shop's display. From the foam core I cut thin strips I made into a grid. To add a touch of whimsy, I added a snow-covered roof and chimney. Each box was lined with a different fabulous paper, and then the edges were gilded in gold. It was a delicate four-foot-high by three-foot-wide by two-inch-deep dollhouse of wonder. John and I carefully transported it over to the shop and put it in place, then scavenged the shop to find the perfect treats to fill up the cubes.

Every other shop in town was flocked with garland and tinsel and twinkly lights. Ira, God bless him, had always made Christmas in the shop seem sweet and magical and homespun. But now that I was the one going through boxes of decorations, it became very apparent that Samuel's was in need of some upgrades. We cleaned out all the old stuff Ira had held on to. He saved everything: ribbon, magazines with ideas for the shop, props for window displays. One night, we found a stash of very old candy nutcrackers. John held one up and lovingly impersonated Ira saying, "You never know when you might need it again." We smiled as we remembered our friend.

I ran out to Home Depot and went full Griswold, filling a shopping cart with large globe string lights and bright blue and red shiny garland. I found ornaments as big as my head and large magnets so we could hang them from our ceiling fans. Signs and Santas and mini-trees overflowed from the back of my SUV as I rolled back up to the shop. John, Vincent, and a few other teenagers pulled an all-nighter as we decorated the shop.

Since Andy, Phoebe, Julie, and Paul spent the week in the city where their kids were in school, their role in our new operation was to check out the layout and functionality of shops there and find exclusive products (Megpies were a Phoebe find and are now at Starbucks, but we had 'em first!). Then they'd come up every weekend and assess all the work John and I were doing. Our friends had gambled on Jeffrey's whim, and so even though we *still* didn't own Samuel's, I wanted them to see the bright, shiny future that lay ahead of us.

The workload was nuts. We had to pack thousands of bags of candies for Sinterklaas and start filling hundreds of holiday mail-order boxes. Everyone in town who had been moved by Ira's life called the shop wanting to send gift boxes, just as Jeffrey and I had done the year before. The store was still in massive debt and couldn't afford to hire holiday help, so an army of volunteers made up of Ira's friends marched in and rolled up their sleeves. Meredith, who has a bunch of kids to whom Ira was an uncle, came in practically every day and helped us bag candy, measuring the pieces out to a fraction of a gram, carefully placing a logo sticker on the front and a description label on the back, then tying a tidy bow at the top.

Our chocolate bark maker, Celeste, works at an accounting firm and has a little boy the same age as Gus. Ira was family to her, and as soon as she heard we needed help, she rallied. I have no idea how she works a full-time job, takes care of her family, and still finds time to make mountains of chocolate.

It was beautiful chaos. We packed into the tiny store a lot of women, a lot of boxes, a lot of caffeine and craft brown tissue paper, and a constellation of candy and customers. I could hear John talking to customers—praising Donna's cookies, giving someone a sample of Celeste's bark, asking one of our regulars, Heinz, about his family. Or asking the high schoolers about their teachers, whom John knew from his days as a student at Rhinebeck High. I smiled to myself, remembering how we'd been unsure whether John was up for the role. But now I could see that he truly was the Candy Man.

We worked way after dark and long after closing, Christmas music rollicking in the background. We listened to Ira's playlist over and over during that week after Thanksgiving—songs he personally chose, burned onto a CD, and played on that monstrosity of a stereo perched atop the milk fridge. John took stock of everything around us. "Ira would have loved all this! I wish he could see it."

"I know," I said, feeling a little guilty. None of us had known the financial danger the shop had been in. Had Ira ever mentioned it, all these same volunteers would have shown up to help. We would have donated the decorations, solicited mail orders to help pay off the bills. It would have been a very different story for our friend. The idea of his carrying that burden with only young John to confide in made me very sad.

Elvis's "Blue Christmas" came on and the group fell quiet. It's funny how you can hear a song your whole life and it's just words and music. And then one day that same song can take on a whole new meaning and knock the breath out of you. "Blue Christmas" is Ira's song now.

In a flurry of activity, we finally got a closing date. Andy called with the news. "Hil, can you go to the signing as our representative tomorrow?" It was scheduled for 5 p.m., just a couple of short days before the biggest weekend of the year in Rhinebeck—Sinterklaas.

I was on pins and needles. Andy had taught me so much about business over the previous six months. He'd been well-versed and thoughtful about all the financial decisions we'd made as a group. His asking me to go to the signing felt like a show of confidence. I was leaving my teen-drama cocoon and emerging a business-lady butterfly.

All that time during negotiations we hadn't been able to talk about what we were up to because it wasn't a done deal yet. But these were my friends and neighbors; I couldn't contain my excitement. The morning of the signing I sent Gus's preschool teacher Ms. Patty a letter. The kids had a field trip to the hospital the next day, and I was signed up to chaperone. "Signing the paperwork on our ownership of Samuel's tonight! If you could pass along to the other parent chaperones that they are all welcome to come in, I'd love to treat them to coffee."

I picked Gus up at school, dropped him off with Jeffrey at home, got good-luck kisses from my boys, and then put on my big girl business blazer and headed into town for the meeting. The law office was just down the street from the shop. I met our lawyer, John Marvin, over there as well as Ira's husband, also named John, and his legal team. Sitting down at a long, shiny conference table, there was certainly an element of awkwardness. Everyone wanted to claim Ira, and ownership over the shop had been a tug-of-war between friends and family and John-the-husband. But then, John-the-husband pulled out a gift bag from under the table.

"I just thought you should have this," he said to me. Inside was Ira's teddy bear, the one he had used in the Sinterklaas pageant every year. I stroked the bear's soft fur and smiled.

"This means a lot to me, John."

The meeting was long. Technical. Arduous. But we had done it. Samuel's was ours.

The moment it was over I raced to Rhinebeck Wine and Liquor right across the street from Samuel's. The store was bustling with holiday activity. The owners of the shop are Joe and Kim Curthoys, parents to one of Gus's classmates. "Good news?" they asked as they rang up a bottle of champagne.

"Great news!" It was so nice to finally say out loud that we had bought the shop.

"Well, let's make sure we give you the local merchant discount." I grinned and waved goodbye, and then raced across the street.

John Traver met me out front. "Is it a done deal?"

Holding up the bottle, I squealed, "We gotta take a picture!"

The next day the real work began. To my delight, all the parents from school showed up in support: Tara, whom I always parked next to and gossiped with in the back of the parking lot; Piper, whose family owned several buildings in town; Allison, who taught yoga; Hallie, who always wore a megawatt smile; Joe, the dad of one of Gus's buddies; and countless other parents. To go from living in a place where your neighbor doesn't recognize you after five years to this? It justified every decision Jeffrey and I had made. It confirmed that I was exactly where I was supposed to be.

Our group of friends-now-business-partners had been emailing like mad about all sorts of details—new products, store hours, revenue, giveaways for the festival that weekend. I sent out an email. We all had big ideas about how to make this the best Sinterklaas ever. But real life was full of practicalities.

Thu, Dec 4, 2014, 4:28 PM

Hi guys!

So before I get into a store update, I just gotta throw this out there. I don't want to be Buzzkill Burton, but I feel pretty strongly that all the "new stuff" needs to wait until after Sinterklaas.

The logistics of just standard operating on such a big day are hard enough as is. We have JT and two employees working that day, and it's their first Sinterklaas Festival in the shop. It's tight quarters. Our counter space is nonexistent. And the free samples that are already planned are for items like bark and the locally made candy canes.

I know everyone is excited, but we're in "stabilization" mode right now. I think the best thing we can do as new owners is just be around, maybe in shifts. Every day, folks have been coming in asking about the ownership, and starting yesterday we could finally tell them. It's been a warm response, and all people wanna do is shake hands and say congrats.

I was just telling Jeff that we had a really wonderful interaction today. A man named Blair came in and asked what was going on. I explained our group to him and how we are preserving Ira's life's work, and he told me he was a good friend of Ira's. He had been in the shop two days before Ira passed, and had not been back since. It was too hard. But he was so lovely and thanked us and said he was happy to be a customer again, knowing the store was being loved.

Okay, on to store business . . .

Today was an education in the shop. I've inventoried 95 percent of the product on our shelves, learned prices, organized some software that allows for a quick search of prices. JT is excited about that.

Most everything is bagged and priced. Mail-order packages are being assembled and the first ones go out tomorrow. Our FedEx account has been reinstated.

Ira's mom called. She had no idea what has been going on. JT told her about us and she cried. She's very happy her boy is being honored.

Today doing inventory I asked if they were called gummie fish or Swedish fish, and they said we should call them Paul's fish since he buys them a lot. Cute.

I have to go back tomorrow. Let me know if there is anything you want me to look into while I'm there, but Oh My God! We can finally celebrate. And at Sinterklaas no less!!! A few minutes before the parade, they call out "last call" for hot chocolate and push everyone out of the store so we can all watch the parade together. Then they head back in a few minutes before the finale to get started again and stay open till 10 p.m.

Dinner tomorrow would be great.

XOXOXOX

h

Sinterklaas had taken on an entirely new meaning to all of us now that we were store owners. Andy showed up early in the morning and hobnobbed with customers until it was time to judge the teddy bear contest. Along with John, they did their best to fill Ira's shoes and gifted every kid with a certificate and chocolate bear. Andy and Phoebe had a knack for communicating with the clientele on the weekends, creating casual conversation to get feedback that would inform our direction in the shop. The Rudds took the afternoon shift, shaking hands and being the outgoing, warm people that they are.

I was on evening shift. In our months working together, John and I had taken on the subconscious habit of dressing alike. Decked out in our matching plaid shirts, we stirred hot chocolate by the gallon, shared the good news of ownership with all who came in, and plotted the special event that was going to take place in the shop later that evening. A few weeks before, John had pulled me aside. "Hilarie, I got a call today from a lady in town. Her daughter was a really big *One Tree Hill* fan." He paused for a second, looking a little sheepish. "Well, her daughter's boyfriend wants to propose to her during Sinterklaas at the candy store, and she wondered whether you could be there." I could see how much he hated asking, but I was more than happy to do the favor for him. And now tonight was the night!

Jeff and Gus met me at Osaka for a quick family dinner. "How's it going over there?" Jeff asked.

"It's a zoo! The marriage proposal is happening right before the parade, so I'll text everyone when the guy gets there. They're cute kids. The bride's mom is a regular customer."

I raced back over to the shop and hung out in the back office with the hopeful fiancé, feeling a little giddy to be part of someone's big romantic moment. Our two high school employees were positioned to capture the whole affair with their smartphone cameras. With the future groom and his father nervously chatting in the back, John and I eyeballed the front door, waiting for the mother of our unsuspecting romantic victim to come in. I spotted the mom through the big front window and tucked back into my hiding place. From out by the cash register I heard John greet her extra loudly, "It's so good to see you!"

She was equally as loud and I was *dying*. "Good to see you John! This is my daughter. She's a big *One Tree Hill* fan, and we were just curious whether Hilarie was around."

"Oh yes, she's just in the back," John said. "Hilarie? Are you free?" His acting was pretty bad, but the daughter had no idea. I popped my head out, desperately trying to keep a straight face.

"What's up, bud?"

"There's someone out front who wants to say hi." I ducked under the counter and gave her a hug.

"It's so nice to meet you. Your mom has told me a lot about you." She gave her mother one of those looks a girl can only give her mother, but then went on to talk about the show, how happy she was that we had bought the shop, and the people we knew in common. It became clear she had no idea what was going on.

"Hold on," I said. "We know someone else in common. And I think he wants to talk to you." Confusion washed over her face. I yelled into the back, "Hey buddy, can you join me out here?"

Her boyfriend emerged, shaking, and though I don't know whether he'd admit it, I noticed he was a bit teary-eyed. Everyone in the shop stopped what they were doing. Getting down on one knee, he told her how much he loved her and pulled out the ring. She was so happy, she couldn't speak.

"Is that a yes?" I asked as she made excited sounds, her hands covering her mouth. She nodded her head YES! as he stood up, and the entire shop broke out into applause.

After the proposal, I met up with Jeff and our friends in front of the store for the parade, the guys holding the kids up on their shoulders as we all huddled together for warmth. A gorgeous new polar bear mascot danced along the parade route.

"When did they get him?" I yelled over the pulse of the drum line.

"This year!" John yelled back. "They're calling him Ira." I smiled. Ira was all around us.

Jeff had spent so much of the year away that when he was offered a job to do a TV show in LA, I wasn't exactly happy.

"Babe, I spoke with the producers," he told me. "They want you to come be on the show too. I told them the only way I'd do it is if they kept my family together." It was thoughtful that he wanted me along for the ride. But you know what's gross? Riding coattails. There wouldn't be a lot for me to do. Over the course of the season I'd pop in every third episode and yell at Grace Gummer as some high-strung government agency bitch. And I'd get to work with Tyler Hilton for a third time. But it was clearly a bone the producers were throwing Jeff to get him to agree to take the role.

I was torn. We had so much on our plate with the farm and the shop. And though I was happily doing the work it took to get them up and running, I wasn't getting paid for either of those jobs. The fact was, I'd barely worked for pay since we'd made the full-time move upstate. Doing an easy job could help us out financially. And then there was the fact that I most certainly couldn't get pregnant with Jeff across the country.

At that point, I was starting to get a hair anxious that I wasn't pregnant yet. Gus was our magical baby who had been created quickly and with no trouble as Jeffrey and I fell in love. It had been amazing. After he was born, I thought, *Problem solved.* I had a kid.

I had the best, easiest labor of anyone I know. I believed that my body was meant to do this, and all the stuff I'd been told about having a hard time getting pregnant was bullshit.

But we were approaching a year of trying and . . . nothing.

So while I wasn't super thrilled about it, the decision was made. We'd go to LA to shoot the show.

Jeff went out ahead of us. My character wouldn't appear till later in the season anyway, so it gave me time to tie up loose ends and handle things at Samuel's that needed immediate attention. Such as the sign.

The sign out front was a large wood square with burgundy checkerboard painted on. In black letters across the diagonal, it said SAMUEL'S. Andy, who owned a successful marketing firm in the city, pointed out the obvious. "It doesn't say anywhere *what* we sell." We decided as a group to elaborate on the name. "Samuel's Sweet Shop" informed passersby that we were peddling sugar, and it had a nice ring to it.

We ended up leaving up the string of large Christmas lights, as they added much-needed brightness to the shop. But what we needed most was a logo that didn't "look like a pizza box," as Phoebe put it, and a new color scheme.

To tide us over, John and I decorated the place for Valentine's Day. Winters can be notoriously slow for the small mom-and-pop shops in town, so we wanted to inject some excitement into Samuel's.

"Let's put a kissing booth in our window," I said to John one day.

Stringing up hearts I'd made from wax paper and shavings from Gus's crayons, we hung a banner across the top of our window that said KISSING BOOTH in big red hand-printed letters. I'd made it from a roll of freezer paper, laid out across my kitchen island.

When Jeff was home, he and I took a photo in front of it. "You think you can get other people in town to do the same?" I asked John.

"Of course I can," he answered. I liked his attitude. Soon, high school kids and couples from town were taking advantage of the photo op.

I went over to the shop one day and took photos from literally every angle—interior, exterior—because I wanted everything captured as it was. Then I came home and whited out all the burgundy and made copies. With Gus's little set of paints, I painted in all the trim and floors and exterior architecture with various color schemes. Andy had wanted something a bit more yellow and happy. And the Rudds were partial to Americana red, white, and blue vibes. Scanning them and sending them out, I thought there was a clear winner. Using a warm yellow-tinged cream as our base color, and cherry red, with a vintage turquoise blue, that rendering of the shop popped. It had enough of what everyone wanted to be a nice compromise.

Gus and I got a house/puppy/alpaca sitter to keep an eye on things while we shuttled back and forth from LA. A week out there, three weeks at home, and so on and so forth until April. "Just stay for the month," Jeff suggested. "Gus is in preschool. It's gonna get so much harder to travel when he's older." He was right. Gus and I could explore things in LA that would rival what he was learning at preschool. We hit up the La Brea Tar Pits, the history museum, the Griffith Observatory, the Gene Autry museum. We spent Easter out in the desert of La Quinta where Jeff's dad and stepmom lived.

Jeff and I liked working together. We liked knowing all the same people and comparing notes at the end of the day. I liked that he made everyone laugh, and he would tell me that he was proud of me for how I conducted myself on set. Things were going so well that we didn't really have plans to go home. Sure, there was stuff I could be doing to prep the garden, but I'd lived in New York long enough to know that anything planted before May was just frost bait and destined to die.

Then, late one night in mid-April we got a frantic call from our house sitter. She was in tears. "Something's wrong with Bisou! She's having these seizures!"

Bisou Morgan had been with Jeff for eighteen years. She had been the runt of the litter, far too young to be away from her mama when Jeff bought her out of a cardboard box off some grifter kids in Venice, California. She had seen him through failure and through success, through major relationships and solitude. She had been to almost every set he ever worked on. As much as I loved her, I knew this news was gut-wrenching for Jeff. What made it even harder was that the show still needed him in LA; he wouldn't be able to easily get back home.

"I'll go," I told him. The next day, Gus, our babysitter Doris, and I were on a plane back to New York. Shout-out to Doris. Besides the baby nanny who helped us out the first few months of Gus's life, I'd never had a nanny. But whenever I worked in LA, I called Doris, who was a young woman of nineteen when I met her. She took care of Gus during the first Christmas movie I did. From then on, any time a short job popped up, I looked forward to calling Doris. Years later, she knew what Bisou meant to us.

The next week at home, Doris minded Gus while I took Bisou to an endless series of vet appointments. After multiple vets and scans, we discovered that she had a huge tumor in her brain. She had been doing strange things for a while, like knocking down the trashcan and acting weird in her sleep. Jeff and I had just chalked such things up to her being eighteen years old, but they turned out to be symptoms of a much bigger problem.

For the next week, I'd get Gus ready for school in the morning and Doris would drive off with him; then I'd load Bisou—who was a hefty old gal—into the truck and head down to Yonkers for radiation treatments. In the waiting room, I'd hold her in my lap and just cry. She was so good. And gentle. And smart. She was the animal that taught me to really love animals. And how was I gonna know I was pregnant again without our sweet girl to let us know? She had known I was pregnant with Gus even before I knew. One day she had curled up at my feet and wouldn't let Jeff come anywhere near me. He was flabbergasted.

"This is my girl. This is my dog."

"Well, not anymore. Apparently, now she loves me."

The radiation was a risky procedure, but Jeff was locked into professional obligations and I *had* to keep her alive. After multiple rounds of treatment, the doctor had great news. "The tumor has shrunk! This lady might very well live another eighteen years."

Bijou seemed to be back to her old self. She was brighter and moving more easily. Jeff and I shared a collective sigh, and meanwhile, sweet Doris was able to enjoy seeing the East Coast for the first time. "What kind of tree is that?" she asked me one day. Looking over to where she was pointing, I answered, "A maple."

"What are those pink things on it?"

It took me a moment to understand what she was asking. But Doris, who had lived her entire life in California surrounded by palms and succulents, had never seen a fully blooming spring before. She was asking about the tree buds.

"I love it!" she cried.

I loved sharing the farm with Doris. She had known our family through the various phases of our life—LA, cabin, and now Mischief Farm. Her enthusiasm meant a lot. Once everything settled down, though, Doris headed back to LA, and I set out to do my May planting.

On the Friday before Mother's Day, I saw something was wrong with Bisou. It was a special day, the anniversary of the day I had met Jeff (and Bisou). After I'd taken Gus to school, I stopped in the house before heading off into the garden. I immediately saw something wasn't right with Bisou. Her abdomen looked unnaturally large. She was having trouble moving again. Jeff was on a plane to the UK to do a convention, which meant he was unreachable. I loaded Bisou into the truck and raced over to the emergency clinic. They did a draw on her stomach. Internal bleeding.

I called the clinic in Yonkers, and they told me to come down right away, but there was nothing they could do either. After overcoming the brain tumor, Bisou's organs were failing. "We can stabilize her by removing the blood in her stomach cavity, but it's going to come back within forty-eight hours," the vet told me.

Once Jeff had landed, I called him from the waiting room.

"What's wrong?" he said, knowing that I make phone calls only when it's important.

"Honey, you need to come home."

Jeff did two full days' worth of photos and autographs in one day, not wanting to disappoint the people who had traveled from all over to see him. Then he got on the earliest flight he could and arrived the morning of Mother's Day. Bisou lay in our bed. Her eyes were tired. She weakly thumped her tail when she saw Jeff. Gus was so happy to see his dad, it was difficult to balance that happiness against the loss of our old lady. We grilled steak for her and fed her ice cream. And on that warm May day, we lay in the sunny grass and let her rub her face in the sea of dandelions.

Our vet came over in the afternoon. We wanted Gus to be present, to understand the gravity of life and also that death doesn't have to be scary—it can be loving. We were all together, and Jeffrey cried and I cried and I watched as Gus made himself cry.

I reached over and said, "Awww, honey. You don't have to do that."

"But I want Dad to know how much I care."

It was a very gentle goodbye. It was Gus's most profound encounter with loss, since he'd been too little to understand when Ira had died a year before.

After, we went for a family walk just to get out of the house and clear our heads. We did a lap around the farm. Gus, in his four-year-old wisdom, said, "Hey, can we rename the dandelions Bisoulions?"

He had figured out a way to make it better. Walking with Gus through this experience showed me how exposing kids to rough stuff when they're younger helps to strengthen their coping skills. They're not blindsided by the pain and grief. They understand that adversity and death are just a part of the cycle.

That dog was magic.

Dandelion Wine

Ray Bradbury's book *Dandelion Wine* is my favorite book of all time. I picked up my first copy in a tiny bookshop in the West Village when I was nineteen. I own first-edition copies and autographed copies. I keep multiple copies in my basement at all times to hand out at a moment's notice and have gifted the book to more people than I can count. I own a wine label from Bradbury Vineyards signed by Ray himself. I possess glass paperweights with whole dandelion puffs encased inside, and I drink dandelion tea at least four times a week. All of this is to say, the sense memory that dandelions provide is dear to me.

For hundreds of years, these vibrant plants have been regarded as medicine, an elixir for the body and mind. Bradbury's book is an homage to the small town he grew up in, a collection of short stories woven together through the eyes of two young brothers. That lifestyle is what I always wanted for my children and for my family. When I found Rhinebeck, I found the town I'd always pictured in my mind. So naturally, making my own dandelion wine was a priority when I moved to the farm.

Each spring our fields become a sea of golden flowers, signaling that winter's spell has been broken. That's the kind of magic you want to bottle up and save for a gray day. Now our family calls dandelions Bisoulions, and our concoction is a serum of love and family and earth and hope. It's our spring ritual, collection day falling between Jeff's birthday at the end of April and Mother's Day in May. The recipe changes a bit from year to year. A touch more local honey. Lemons to remember that first night Jeff and I met. But it always tastes like sunshine and hard work.

Dandelion Wine

1 gallon yellow dandelion petals (pinch them out and remove all the green)

1 gallon water

2 oranges (zest and juice)

2 lemons (zest and juice)

1-inch piece of ginger root

Add-ins, to taste: Honey, golden raisins, rose petals, cinnamon, clove berries—anything that makes you think of summer!

3 pounds sugar

1 packet wine yeast (you can buy champagne yeast online)

Collect 1 gallon of petals from fully bloomed dandelions, pinching the petals out of the green sepals. (The greens hold much of the bitterness typically associated with dandelions.) Put the petals in an extra-large stainless steel stock pot. Bring water to a boil. Pour 1 gallon boiling water over the petals. Make sure all the petals are covered, put a large dish towel over the top, and let the mixture sit for three days. Stir once a day with a wooden spoon.

After three days, strain the water from the flowers. Lay out cheesecloth and scoop out a bunch of the soggy petal mix. Twist the cheesecloth up to squeeze all the excess liquid into the pot. Repeat until you have drained all the summertime magic from Every. Single. Petal.

I put the used-up petals into my garden at this point. Not sure they do any good, but it feels like good karma to return them from whence they came.

(continued)

Add to the pot the orange and lemon zest and juice, ginger, and any other special add-in ingredients to make it your own. Then slowly add the sugar, stirring constantly as you bring the mixture to a low boil for 20 minutes. Let liquid cool to room temperature.

In a separate, small bowl, mix the yeast with ½ cup warm water. Let it sit for 5 minutes to proof. Stir the yeast mixture into the pot of dandelion liquid. Filter out any solids through a fine-mesh strainer as you distribute the wine mix into sterilized, airtight jars. Make sure to leave plenty of headroom in the jar so nothing bursts as it ferments!

You'll see bubbles form in the jar as your wine ferments from six days to three weeks. Once the fermentation stops, filter the liquid through a cheesecloth-lined strainer as you pour it into sterilized glass bottles. Put a balloon over the top of each bottle to keep an eye on any further fermentation. If it remains deflated for more than twenty-four hours, the process is done. Cork the bottle. Let sit for six months, preferably somewhere cool and dark like a basement. Then, just as the chill of autumn starts creeping in, your reminder of warmer days is ready to keep you company.

Jeff headed back to LA, and the producers asked whether I'd come back as well, but my heart wasn't in it. I couldn't stand the fact that things had gone sideways with Bisou while I was gone. This farm? The shop? I had made a commitment to them. So while Jeff wrapped up the season, I put on my hardware-store pants and got back to work.

Samuel's had no idea what hit it. I painted everything. I painted the bathroom pink and made it very feminine, because I find that it's harder to leave things dirty if they're super girly looking. One of the high school kid employees took one look and quibbled, "What the hell is this?"

"It's a little reminder to put the seat down," I teased. John laughed.

We needed a better display for our coffee. Andy and Phoebe and Julie had scoured every roaster in the city. It was important to us that we use a New York company, and it had to have the best coffee ever. They settled on Toby's Estate, and the Toby's people were wonderful, coming up to the shop to train our staff on how to make the perfect cup of coffee. Mechanics fixed all of our equipment, so we were firing on all pistons. Now we needed that coffee set up in a way that felt special. Naturally, I headed straight over to Hoffman's Barn Sale to see John's folks.

"Whatcha looking for today?" Roger asked.

"Oh hell, I don't ever really know until I see it. You got any tables?"

Sure enough, Roger had two pedestal tables, perfect for the sitting area toward the front of the shop. And then I found a perfect 1950s enamel-top table with curvy chrome legs and a cream-colored enamel with delicate red scrolling details. I loved the idea of our coffee looking like it was set up in Grandma's house. We wanted our customers to feel at home, and even with our new, brighter color scheme, the design fell in line with the original rustic environment Ira had cultivated. "I'll take 'em all!"

I painted the pedestal tables our vintage blue color, and Gus helped me add touches of cream and red. Just as spring was blooming, Samuel's was waking up with bursts of color.

The shelf that runs along the top of the store with Ira's collected memorabilia was always a feast for the eyes. We wanted to add some of our own things to the collection. Andy offered his old tin *Welcome Back, Kotter* and *Dukes of Hazzard* lunchboxes. One day Kim Curthoys from the liquor store across the street came in with her old lunchboxes. "I'd like to add this to the collection and be part of it," she told us.

Just like that, Samuel's became a quilt that we all added on to. People were willing to try new things to help. We had our morning coffee people and our afternoon coffee people, so a caterer in town started making wraps and sandwiches, allowing us to capture the lunch crowd. We enlisted someone else to make fresh juices. Donna, our retired postmaster, began baking a couple dozen cookies every week. She's so talented that when we started promoting her cookies, we needed hundreds and hundreds of them. So she went from baking as a retirement hobby to a full-time gig. My favorite are her artist cookie packs. They have two cookie sections: one with cookies covered in white royal icing with the black outline of a shape to color (I love the butterflies), and the other with cookies having a rectangle of the same royal icing but with dollops of food coloring that act like watercolor paints. We sold the cookies with little paintbrushes that you could dip in water and use to decorate your own cookie. The kids loved it.

I soon got a crash course in local rules and protocol. The building manager, Bill, had done a gorgeous job of painting the shop with our new cheerful color scheme. But out front sat a beleaguered bench, unpainted for years and a bit rickety, like a shipwreck parked in front of our plate-glass window. I picked up a pint of our red color, tightened all the bench's bolts, and set about putting lipstick on that pig. Everyone walking by commented on how nice Samuel's was looking. The happy red bench was literally the cherry on top.

The next day when I came into the shop, John said, "Hil, there's an issue."

It turns out you can't paint just whatever you want, whenever you want to. The town claimed the bench was their property. "But they weren't taking care of it!" I argued.

"They're going to send the mayor over to take a look at everything. See what we can and can't do."

The mayor? I freaked out. Was I in a lot of trouble?

Heath, the mayor at the time, came over the next day. "It looks great!" he said, surveying all the work we'd done.

"I'm sorry about the bench," I offered up. "I had no idea it was the town's responsibility and not ours. It was just in such bad shape. But if you guys want to put a new bench there . . ." I didn't even finish.

"The bench is fine," Heath said. "You're doing a good thing. Let me know if you need any help."

Huh. That was easy. Too easy. But it prompted a crash course in local protocol. I learned that every sign has to be approved, you can't place new seating on the sidewalks, nighttime lighting must be uncolored light and must come from a historically appropriate fixture. And on and on. I knew I was bound to mess up again, but at least I had the mayor on my team. So next time, when I inadvertently planted flowers where I shouldn't have, the town gently told me to ease up, and let it slide.

Planting those flowers, I made a new friend, Mari Bird, an interior designer who had been very good friends with Ira. After he passed, Janice moved her antique shop, which had been next door to Samuel's, to another location, and Mari took over the next-door space and opened a beautiful boutique that sells resort wear. We planted flowers outside the shops together, and Mari would come over and keep me company while I painted Samuel's. As Mari and I started sprucing up our storefronts, we watched as a couple doors down another business got a fresh paint job. The beautification bug was contagious.

Another beautification project of mine didn't go so well. We have a tiny median between the side of our building and the driveway that leads into the CVS parking lot, so I asked the CVS manager whether it would be okay to put in a garden and some benches so our customers could sit outside when the weather was nice. "Sure, do whatever you want," he said. "We don't maintain it." But no sooner had I started digging than the owners of the property sent us a cease-and-desist letter. I offered to buy this piece of land from them, or even rent it. They refused every offer point blank. Then, I discovered that twenty years back, Ira had opposed the building of the CVS because he believed in the mom-and-pop way of doing things. In fact, a little pharmacy in town had ended up going out of business once CVS opened.

You win some, you lose some.

I gave up and went to see Pam and Roger at Hoffman's Barn Sale, where I found a big old door and hung pots with colorful flowers cascading out of its windows. If we mounted it to the side of our building, then *technically* it wasn't on the median and I could skirt around the cease and desist. As I was painting and gardening, a small group of old men watched me from across the street where they sat perched in front of Bread Alone. They didn't say anything to me, just looked on, I imagine a little skeptically. Then one afternoon when I was almost done, they wandered over and a bearded man told me, "Looks good, kid."

When I was done I hung a little sign that reads: THE IRA GUTNER MEMORIAL GARDEN.

12

Failure is the condiment that gives success its flavor.

—**Truman Capote, "Self-Portrait"**

By the summer of 2015, Samuel's Sweet Shop had found its footing, Gus was thriving, and Jeff and I had found a home, a community, and a way of life that nurtured and sustained us. I wanted to bring another child into this beautiful life we'd carved out.

As a woman, you fight in all these ways: to be treated with respect, to have your body be your own, to make decisions about who can touch you and when and when to have sex and with whom. And then, when you feel like you've fought those battles and won—maybe a little more scarred, but also a little more sure and happy and able to enjoy your body instead of being afraid it will be turned into a vulnerability—it fails you.

A full year after Jeff had announced to the pack of guys in Durango that we were trying to get pregnant, I was spending hundreds of dollars on ovulation tests. I hated those little fucking purple and blue boxes. I was peeing on sticks, tracking my ovulation, checking discharge, even looking at moon cycles. I was reading stuff online—and online can be an awful, dark place. I talked to doctors, and Jeff and I started considering doing fertility treatments.

The show in LA hadn't been picked up for another year, which was unfortunate, but also a relief to me. Jeff got a job on *The Good Wife*, which meant he was in New York City, only a short train ride away.

The summer was idyllic, with Jeremy and Addie Sisto coming back out to visit. We held an epic softball game in the acreage by the house, with the Rudds and Andy and Phoebe and all the kids. Fun fact: Julie Rudd is a serious softball player who does not believe in dumbing the game down for kids. She's hands-down the scariest pitcher I've ever faced.

Summer turned into fall, and you guessed it, I still wasn't pregnant. So I turned everything up to eleven. I had my fertility down to a science. I would pee on a stick, see that I was ovulating, drop Gus off at school, drive to the city to meet up with Jeff, and push myself on that poor man. Then I'd drive home and pick Gus up from school.

It wasn't very romantic, and understandably, Jeff became resistant to the whole situation. He felt like cattle and retreated. For my part, I felt like I'd earned the right to have another baby. I'd been asking for years, and he had agreed the previous year. I was the one who stayed home and took care of the farm and the shop and Gus while he was off working. And it was my body. The least he could do was put out.

We had a hellacious fight in the fall. Jeff was laid up in bed in the city, sick with a cold that had knocked him on his ass. I figured I could kill two birds with one stone. "Well I'm ovulating today, so I'm making you some honey chicken soup and driving it down to you." Gus was at school, so I had exactly the right amount of time to drive down to our rental apartment, feed the man, take advantage of my fertility window, and drive back in time for pickup.

"Dammit Hilarie, I'm sick," he growled. "I'll be home in a few days!"

How the hell did he not understand that in a few days it would be too late? I cried big fat ugly tears. At that point, we were just irritating the shit out of each other. There was no romance; the whole thing had become a science experiment. Jeff wanted me to wine and dine him. He wanted to go on a date. He is a narrative-oriented person, and the narrative of peeing on a stick and rushing to have sex was not attractive to him. He wanted another beautiful story, like how we had lucked into Gus's pregnancy. He'd feel used and wouldn't respond to me, and then I'd feel hurt and rejected. It was a vicious, unhappy cycle.

Every single month that went by felt like a tiny funeral.

I channeled my energy into the farm. One morning Jeff brought in the mail and noticed the Best Made Company catalogue (the go-to source for hip lumberjacks). But that month's cover wasn't a leather-faced Sam Elliott type in flannel. It was a gorgeous blond mastodon-looking cow with horns the size of a Buick.

"Look at that thing!" Jeff said. "I fucking love it!"

Twenty minutes later, I'd found a listing on Craigslist for two Highland cattle in a neighboring state. And two days after that, they were being unloaded in our back pasture.

"This is Alice," the young man said as a silver behemoth slow-walked her way out of the bright-red trailer. "She's gonna give birth in the spring. Don't worry. These are the sturdiest animals on the planet." We had heard stories from Ed about a whole herd of

The Fun of Failure

You have to have fun in the failures, especially when you're reinventing yourself and trying new things. Your failures become your most memorable stories.

I once read a gardening book that suggested planting morning glories next to sunflowers so their pretty tendrils could grow up the sunflower stalks. Instead, the evil morning glories consumed my entire garden. It was a lost year. You couldn't even open the gate. In response, I took a scorched-earth approach, wading into the garden bed with a machete and eventually torching the worst-afflicted part.

On another occasion, I planted the zucchini and yellow squash too close together. The leaves have tiny prickers on them, so you couldn't go into the squash patch without being attacked. Spacing instructions are important.

But it is my Tinkertown fajita fiasco that I remember most fondly. During our New Mexico courtship in the land of enchantment, Jeff and I happened upon the Tinkertown Museum. Above the large entry archway made of random scraps of wheel axles, blue lettering declared, LIVE LIFE AS THE PURSUIT OF HAPPINESS.

I felt like Alice in Wonderland, stepping into a strange and magical world. I put 25 cents into Esmerelda, the fortune teller, and then we checked out the crazy collection of wedding cake toppers, antique tools, hand-carved figures, and elaborate scenes of old Western towns and the circus. Ross Ward had made them and created this whole menagerie. We wound our way through this glorious mishmash of Americana. Pursuit of happiness in the land of enchantment.

That week, Jeff decided to make me his special, delicious pinwheel steak. It's thin steak wrapped up with some other stuff—the recipe is a total mystery to me. A few nights later, I was determined to show Jeffrey what I could do with leftovers; I wanted to prove that I wasn't pretentious or high maintenance. I seasoned the leftover pinwheel beef, sliced up a pile of yellow peppers and onions and sautéed them, then toasted fresh tortillas over the gas burner, flipping them with tongs to make sure they charred just so. Fajitas.

"Smells good," he called out. I served up his plate before fixing my own. Jeff was multiple bites in before I'd begun.

Then I spat out my first bite, yelling, "Don't eat this! It's horrible!" I'd seasoned the meat not knowing that Jeff had soaked it in teriyaki sauce for a full day. The combination tasted like salt and mud.

But Jeff insisted it was good and finished his plate. "They're fine! Just a little bit . . . Tinkertown." Who needs Engagement Chicken?

Poor fella had the worst case of heartburn that night. But failure, and the response I got, made it okay to try things and fail. I felt safe.

Highland cattle that had escaped their fence one day and lived for years in the wild woods of Pleasant Valley.

Behind Alice marched a shy, red-haired cow. "Now this is Hilary," the farmer said. "She got her name cuz we were giving one of my wife's relatives hell. She's got the best temperament." And nothing was truer. That sweet girl let Jeff come right up over and scratch the top of her big shaggy head. It felt powerful to be standing next to these massive creatures. Even though these cattle are largely raised for their meat, I couldn't imagine ever eating one of these majestic animals. *You're safe with us, ladies*, I thought. We name our critters, and once you get a name, you're a pet, and once you're a pet, you can't get eaten. By us, at least. I can't make any promises for the foxes and coyotes.

"We can't call her Hilary," Jeff said later that night.

"Too confusing for you?" I laughed.

"Gus, what are we naming our new lady cow?" Jeff asked.

"And Peggy!" Gus shouted.

Gus was in a big *Hamilton* phase and knew all the words to the songs. In the song that introduces the Schuyler sisters, the women sing their names, "Angelica! Eliza!" and then the youngest says in a nasally childish voice, "And Peggy!" Gus thought the girl's name literally was And Peggy. So our cow became And Peggy.

Jeffrey is so hands-on with the animals, and all of Ed's beautiful baby cows that graze here and get fat all spring and summer end up being like puppy dogs; they're so friendly and outgoing. They like apples and scratches and their sticky sweet-smelling grain at the end of the day.

At the end of summer Ed takes them to the big Dutchess County Fair in town. They always win the beauty pageant awards, like Ms.

Congeniality. Ed Junior handles everything while the cattle are on our land. He's on a tractor all day and sometimes doesn't bother wearing a shirt. It's routine for him to show up with manure all over his pants to check the animals.

Even after Ed's cows were loaded into their barn for the winter, Ed Junior still came by every other day to check Alice. One day he came over looking real nice. He was wearing khakis and a button-down shirt and his hair was combed. Jeff and I privately were atwitter trying to figure out what the occasion was. Church? A *date*? He was standing at the fence looking at Alice to see whether she had started "bagging up"—that's when the udder swells right before a cow gives birth. It looks about as pleasant as it sounds. Then Bandit, the Puerto Rican jungle dog, came up, raised a leg, and pissed all over Junior's pants. Now Bandit might be a jungle dog with few manners, but he had never done that to anyone before. I was mortified.

I ran into the house and got paper towels and was trying to wipe the piss off of Junior's leg while I muttered apologies. He just said, "Hilarie, understand that I work on a dairy farm; I get pissed on every single day."

He laughed. I laughed. Bandit ran in circles. It's true: farm life isn't always pretty, even for us gentleman farmers.

Around this time, an incident with my favorite chicken, Red, crushed me. One of the facts of farm life is death, be it eating the animals you've raised or losing animals to illness or predators. I accept that, for the most part. However, the chickens have such personalities, and Red was so friendly and beautiful. She was from the first batch of chicks we had gotten on Gus's fourth birthday.

Halloween came and went, and the pumpkins were getting soft and mushy. I've learned there's nothing chickens like more than eating the inside of a pumpkin. Jeffrey was chopping wood over in his woodshed, and all the chickens were up in the front yard, pecking at bugs.

My father had told me to keep guinea hens around to eat ticks. Being out here surrounded by trees and deer, ticks are no joke; Lyme disease is a big deal. So we ordered six guinea hens from Ed Hackett. "Are you sure you want those things?" he asked me. "They're pretty awful."

I said, "Yeah. They're gonna get the ticks."

"All right, whatever you want, kid." So we got six cute little spotted chicks, and very quickly, as they got older, I realized these things are the devil. They make the most god-awful noise—a warbly squawk that's like a mix between a turkey call and the sound of something dying. They're really dumb and are the ugliest, buzzardy-looking birds. As they get older, they lose all the feathers on their head and grow a horn on top of it, like a unicorn.

While the chickens were grazing in the front yard, I heaved a giant pumpkin down near the chicken houses, and just as I swung it into the air, a guinea hen ran out of nowhere screaming bloody murder. It frightened all the chickens, sending them running back toward their houses. As the pumpkin arced in midair, I saw Red in its path, and there was nothing I could do to stop it. The pumpkin landed with a huge thud on top of Red.

I ran down that hill so fast and pulled that huge Cinderella pumpkin off of my chicken. She wasn't dead, but given the size of the pumpkin, she must have been bleeding internally, and her leg and a wing looked kind of weird. In the back of my brain hope fluttered—*Maybe she'll pull through. The pumpkin* was *really soft.* By this point all the other birds were feasting on the damn pumpkin as I held Red in my arms like an infant. She looked at me and her eyeballs were going crazy, and I just started crying and carried her over to Jeffrey saying, "I messed up. I messed up. I think I killed Red." And in the midst of telling him this, her body convulsed and then fell limp. I had killed my favorite chicken.

We took Red down to the old tree where the Mischief graves are, and Jeff dug a hole and we buried her. He put a huge stone over her grave.

I left to pick up Gus from school, and when we got home Jeff wasn't there. I brought Gus into the house and gave him a snack, and then Jeff came rolling back in his pickup truck with a flock of Reds—six of them. He had raced over to the feed store and told Ed what happened, which caused everyone in the store to crack up laughing. I get it, she was just a chicken, but I had named her, fed her, and kept her safe and warm. Still, every Halloween when we get our pumpkins, people tease, "Watch her. She's gonna kill something with those things!"

Alice

Our cabin

Gus shortly after
he was born

My brother John and me taking down a popcorn ceiling at my parents' house, preparing me for all the Mischief Farm renovations

Bisou with the "Bisoulions" we named after her

Gus with Tom Turkey

Jeff and Bill Paxton

Jeff and his donkey, Paxton, named after Bill

Painting of Ira
by Tom Cale

Gus living up to his "Lonesome Dove" namesake at the cabin

Alexander

Jeffrey and me
in front of the
Kissing booth at
Samuel's

Mischief headstone

Gus with birds in our bathroom

My "boyfriend"
Ed Hackett
at the fair

Our last day
with Bisou

Our donkeys Ally
and Loretta

Beginnings of the Ira Gutner Garden

Trying to get rid of morning glories in the garden

Out to dinner with the Rudds, Ostroys, Kemps, and Hacketts

Picking dandelions on George's first Mother's Day

Mountain man
and George

George wearing Queen
Anne's lace

Astor fundraiser with Tyler
Hilton, Clayne Crawford,
Michael Raymond-James,
and Mary Stuart Masterson,
2018

The Astor Ladies: Lawrie Firestone,
Kate Kortbus, and Donna Faraldi

Dad and helpers

Gus and Paxton

The girl alpacas

Happy girls

Redhead cow

John Traver and me at
Teddy Bear Beauty Pageant,
SinterKlaas

Pumpkin patch,
2018

Me and
George
at the
wedding

Gus dancing at our wedding reception

The best moment: exchanging vows with my Jeffrey

I can, with one eye squinted,
take it all as a blessing.

—**Flannery O'Connor,**
in *The Habit of Being*:
Letters of Flannery O'Connor

I woke up one morning shortly after Thanksgiving with the tingling in my chest that signaled my hormones were in motion. The double stripe showed up on the pregnancy test almost as soon as I'd peed on it. I sat in the bathroom and thanked the universe. Every day after that felt like a gift.

I wanted to surprise Jeffrey with the news for Christmas, so for a month I kept the pregnancy secret from everyone. We went to Sinterklaas and I judged the Teddy Bear Beauty Pageant. We took Gus into the city to see Santa at Macy's. All the pressure I had been putting on our relationship dissipated. The three of us just wandered around New York the way Jeffrey and I had done when I found out I was pregnant with Gus. I loved the press of people, the rush, the way Christmas blossomed out of every cement crevice— the wreaths and trees being sold on street corners, the Salvation Army bells ringing, the festive shop windows. I loved looking up and seeing the Christmas trees lit up in apartments all over the city. Jeff just thought I was being way more agreeable than usual. We planned on spending Christmas at Mischief Farm, just the three of us. I privately celebrated this, knowing that a new member of our family was on its way and wanting one last holiday to lavish all my attention on Gus, my magic baby.

On Christmas Eve, we went to the candle-lighting service at church, had dinner at our favorite Thai place in town—Aroi—left cookies for Santa, and nestled in. I had placed a joint gift for Jeff and Gus under the tree. The next morning, Gus tore through the wrapping paper. When it was time for the boys to open my gift, I said, "On the count of three. One. Two. Three." And in good-spirited competition, they raced to see who would win. Jeff opened his box first and found Seattle Seahawk baby booties. I filmed his confused face until he looked over to see what Gus had un-wrapped—a "Big Brother" T-shirt. Putting two and two together, big, tough Jeffrey Dean burst into tears. Off camera, you could hear me laughing and Gus saying, "A baby!"

I'd sent our families wrapped photos of the ultrasound with instructions not to open until after I texted them the go-ahead. Everyone was excited. Moms from school sent out the typical "Merry Christmas Ladies" messages in group threads. To which I responded, "I'm pregnant!" In a lovely bit of kismet, another mom friend, Sharagim, announced she was pregnant too. We were due a couple of weeks apart.

Later, when we were lying in bed, Jeff told me, "Hey. I'm sorry I was so . . . resistant to the whole thing. It was just taking so long and not going well. But I want you to know, now that this baby is on the way, I want it so bad. I'm so, so happy." A wave of relief washed over me.

Jeff returned to work after the holiday and we continued to share the good news with everyone around us. I went to work at Samuel's, and customers commented on my glow.

One winter morning in early February Jeffrey was working on *The Good Wife* in the city, and Gus and I were rushing through our morning routine. It was still dark when I let Bandit out and he charged into the inky morning barking at anything that might be out there. Decaf coffee for me, breakfast for Gus, fruit on the counter so we could graze as we wandered in and out. As I was herding Gus out the door, I remembered the new Kissing Booth banner that I needed to drop off at Samuel's later.

By the time we were pulling away from the farm, the morning sun was sharp and bright off the snow. The sky was blue and clear. At a stoplight near school I looked at Gus in the rearview mirror and asked him, "What's more important than being good looking?"

"Being smart," he answered with a broad smile.

"What's more important than being smart?"

"Being kind."

I pulled into the school parking lot. "How do you become a good man like your dad?"

"Be a good kid."

"You got it. Hey Bud, I'm going to go get a picture of the baby today. I'll have it waiting for you when you get home."

I had an early morning appointment with the tech, just a

routine ultrasound; my doctor wasn't even in. I got up on the table, and she smeared the cold gel over my belly and slid the wand across it. She didn't say anything, and I thought, *She's not very outgoing, is she?* She continued staring at the screen, searching for something. Then she tucked the wand away and said, "Could you please have a seat in the waiting room?"

My neck prickled and my hands felt cold.

My baby wasn't alive anymore. I just knew.

I sat in the waiting room for forty minutes. I texted Jeff. He was on set. He couldn't talk. He texted me to be calm and just see what the doctor had to say. Maybe I was jumping to conclusions.

But I knew. A few days earlier I'd been working in the old farmhouse, not doing anything strenuous, just sifting through boxes, when a sharp pain pierced my gut. *That's odd*, I thought. It was unlike anything I'd felt before. But then again, pregnancy is weird—full of aches and pains and strange bodily reactions.

Now in the waiting room all I could think was, *I did this. I should have sat still. I killed my baby.* A nurse came out and told me my doctor was working at a different location that day and wouldn't be in. So I was finally taken to an exam room and introduced to a woman who worked at the healthcare clinic. I didn't know who she was, or what her specific job entailed. But that day she was the ceremonial bearer of bad news. Even in the moment, I felt sorry for her.

I hadn't jumped to the wrong conclusion.

She explained what my options were and then she looked at me and said, "You're going to be okay. This happens to lots of people."

I knew that, but I didn't say anything to her. I didn't stop at the front desk on my way out; I just pushed myself out toward the car. The color had been sapped from the sky and the air had turned to gauze. Even putting one leg in front of the other was impossibly hard.

I sat in the car in the parking lot for a while, afraid to drive. Afraid to move. My phone began ringing.

"What did the doctor say?" Jeff asked.

"She's dead." I'd heard the steady rhythm of our baby's heart just ten days before. We had already chosen a name. What had I done?

I parked behind the candy store and texted John, asking whether he could meet me out back. I couldn't face anyone. Poor John Traver smiled warmly and said, "Morning, Hilarie. How're you feeling?"

"It's dead. I lost it." John hugged me and didn't say much. In the coming weeks, when customers came in asking about me, he gently shared the news so I wouldn't have to tell it over and over. He checked in on me continually, even though I rarely responded. I didn't go back in the candy store for a long time after that. I knew that everyone there knew. The whole damn town knew I was pregnant, and now everyone would know that I'd lost the baby and they'd come in and check on me, and I just didn't want to see them.

I drove back to the farm. I didn't want to pick up Gus until I had figured out how to navigate this, and there was also still a part of me that was hoping the ultrasound was wrong. Maybe the tech had misread it. Maybe my phone would ring and my doctor would say, "I'm sorry, there was a mistake. Your baby is fine."

But my phone didn't ring.

I sat cross-legged on our couch looking out the window, all of the plants and flowers still and dead and barren under a blanket of snow. It was a Friday, which meant Gus's school had a skiing lesson up at Catamount Mountain, and I needed to take him there. The idea of doing that just a few hours after getting this news seemed unbearable. When I told my mother that I had to take Gus to skiing, she said, "No, Hilarie, stay home."

I called my childhood best friend, Sarah Barnes. An ER nurse, she gave me her earnest opinion. There was no mistake. It happens all the time. I could let it "pass naturally" or have a procedure called a D&C to remove everything. I didn't want to make that decision. I told her about taking Gus to skiing, and she said, "No, Hilarie, stay home."

Jeff called me again from set. I knew he was upset. I stared out at the snowy pasture behind the house where And Peggy and Alice were chewing hay. "I think I'm going to bring Gus home this afternoon," I told him. "I just can't talk to the other moms right now."

"No, no. Honey, if you sit at home, you're going to spin your wheels. Go. Be around other people."

Self-loathing set in so quickly that I didn't recognize it. I was a failure, but I couldn't fail Gus now. So I took him skiing. Two of the women had also had children in Gus's class at Ms. Patty's, and they knew me well enough to see that I was coming apart. Quickly, they, and the other mothers, became a net that caught me.

Tara said, "Hi! You tired?" She was the mother I could be snarky with. My birthday twin, we were both Cancers who felt things deeply and covered that with sarcasm.

"I lost the baby." The words fell out of my mouth. There was nothing else for me to say. I didn't know how to make the announcement with social grace.

Tara is an expert in bereavement—she had literally created *the* website on what to do if you lose a child. She knew exactly what to do and what not to say. "Everyone figures it out their own way."

Sharagim—my pregnancy buddy—is a very popular doctor in town, though she wasn't my doctor at that time. She was good friends with my OB-GYN, and before the conversation got too deep, she sat me down at a back table in the lodge, asked whether I would be alright if she contacted my doctor, and said, "I'm going to take care of you."

You know when it starts to rain, and the first drops hit at random places, drawing your attention from here to there as water splashes the ground? That was the effect as I sat in the back of that lodge and the news traveled from mother to mother.

Tara fed me. She handled Gus's ski equipment. She mothered me. Sharagim said, "Your doctor is going to call you. I've taken Monday off. I'll pick you up, okay?"

That afternoon, my doctor called and told me: "For the future of your having children, for your fertility, I recommend a D&C as quickly as possible. You can absolutely naturally pass the pregnancy, but we would still have to go in and make sure that nothing was left behind. We don't want any scar tissue or anything."

I had to be normal for Gus. So we went to bed early. Jeffrey took the train home after work and arrived late. That weekend was painful. We strategized what to say to Gus. Saturday afternoon we asked Gus to sit next to us in the big leather chair by the fireplace. "Hey, Gus, you know how I told you I was going to the doctor yesterday to check on the baby?"

"Yeah."

"Well, the baby . . ." I fought to keep my voice even and started over again. "Our baby was sick. Something wasn't working right, so rather than putting the baby through some hardship, it got called back to God."

I waited for Gus to cry or ask questions or falter in some way, but instead, he looked at me with his great brown eyes and said, "It's okay. We're going to have one." I gave him a small smile; he had inherited his father's optimism.

On Monday Jeff was back in New York shooting. He was upset that I didn't wait for him to get a day off work to have the procedure. I was upset that he didn't just skip work and stay home.

I put Gus on the school bus and waited for Sharagim. She had taken the day off from her medical practice. As she drove to the hospital, I was overwhelmed with gratitude. We had been friendly in a play-date, dinner-on-weekends kind of way. But this was next level, family-type help.

At the hospital she helped me fill out all the paperwork, and she settled me into my room. She got extra blankets and pillows to make me comfortable. She held my hand as they drew blood and put me under, and when I woke up, hers was the first face I saw. Sharagim bought food and stocked my fridge. She picked Gus up at school and brought him home. And between her and Tara, someone was always checking on me.

When you have a miscarriage, there's no funeral. There's no rite for your grief. You mourn alone, even when entirely surrounded by people. But then two weeks after losing the baby, a friend from high school was killed back home, and I was asked to give part of the eulogy. His family had been dear to me growing up. The world felt out of balance. The grief I'd felt for a life I'd loved for only a few months seemed nothing compared to the thirty-seven years of love my friend's parents were now mourning. They had loved him and nurtured him and accepted him through all his successes and shortcomings.

That was when I began faking it. I lied my whole trip home. "I'm good." "We lost the baby, but I'm okay." "Don't worry about me. I'm a tough girl."

When Jeff got home, we came undone. He and I handle stress and grief very differently. He gets quiet and leaves the room, but I need interaction. I need to talk about it, to sort shit out.

Jeffrey retreated to his garage and chopped so many cords that winter we still have wood from that time in our shed. I bleached my hair. I didn't want to be the same person anymore. I renovated the nursery bathroom, like I'd planned while pregnant. Bill from over at the candy store came and did all the hard stuff, like plumbing and ripping out the old tub/shower shell. I stuck to destroying the old tile. Demo hurt. My joints ached; shards of tile left deep cuts in my hands. It was punishment.

Not long after I had told Jeff I was pregnant, we started the work to add a third bedroom to the house. Now, I retreated into designing the addition that we were building for the baby that was gone. We had talked about whether to go forward with the extension; the foundation hole was already being dug, and Jeffrey was stubbornly optimistic. "We're going to get pregnant again. It'll be fine."

But every day we had a crew of people crawling all over the house, reminding me of what we had lost.

14

Life is not what one lived, but what one remembers
and how one remembers it in order to recount it.

—attributed to Gabriel García Márquez

After the miscarriage I was surrounded by dead-baby flowers, dead-baby books, and lots of boxes of dead-baby tea. I felt like I was drowning in a dead-baby sea. My mother didn't know how to help but knew that I needed her. She sent me a soft bathrobe and a teapot, and I wept for hours on the phone with her. Mostly, she listened as I sorted through all my thoughts and feelings. If I'm angry or upset about something, or even if I'm happy about something, it isn't real until I articulate it. I need a narrative. I guess that's something Jeff and I share. We both need a story to fit into. The Burton ability to turn misfortune into narrative is something I'm grateful that I was taught. It helps me think, *Well, okay, that's just a funny story.* You should hear my father talking about his mother and those damn forsythia bushes.

My sisters-in-law sent me lovely, heartfelt packages. Christina sent me teas and a journal and a letter I cherish. She included

Cheryl Strayed's book *Tiny Beautiful Things: Advice on Love and Life from Dear Sugar*. Christina is a mother. I felt like she understood the toll this sadness was taking on me, and she encouraged me to practice self-care. Jess gave me the book *Reveal: A Sacred Manual for Getting Spiritually Naked* by Meggan Watterson and some other books about the divine feminine. She knew that there was nothing she could say, but everything she wanted to articulate was in those books. Jess has always had an almost psychic ability to understand my inner voice. She is quiet and attuned to what people are *really* saying rather than what they present to the world. I knew her book choices were deliberate, but I couldn't read them for a while because they were dead-baby books.

If people weren't giving me dead-baby gifts, they wanted to tell me dead-baby stories. There's nothing more frustrating than someone saying, "Well, welcome to the club. I've had twelve miscarriages." It seemed as if there was an unspoken competition between the members of this fucked-up sorority. I quickly realized that it is a much bigger club than I knew and that everyone had stories and advice. And as much as I appreciated it, I needed to find my own way.

Tara gave me a book called *Vessels: A Love Story*, by Daniel Raeburn, about his and his wife's experience of a number of miscarriages. His book helped because I couldn't wrap my head around Jeff's side of the story, and he certainly wasn't telling it to me. All I could see was his hiding. He was out in the garage until dinnertime every day. He would come in, eat, help Gus shower, and then disappear for the rest of the night.

I often read social media posts from couples announcing, "Hey, we miscarried but it brought us closer together." I think it's fair to say that miscarriage did not bring Jeffrey and me closer together. We were living in the same space but leading parallel lives. To be honest, most of the time we weren't even living in the same space.

That spring *The Good Wife* was canceled. We had banked on that being a job Jeff would do for a couple of years, one that would keep him in New York City. Then he landed Negan on *The Walking Dead*, and suddenly he would be all the way down in Georgia for the next three to five years.

We were never going to have another child. It had been so hard to get pregnant. I felt like I was pulling teeth trying to coordinate dates when Jeff would be around and I'd be ovulating. It felt like every conversation we had was about having a baby.

He'd ask, "What do you want for dinner?"

I'd say, "A baby."

"Hey, what do you want to do this weekend?"

I'd say, "Have a baby."

We tried to fill the house with life. Right before Gus's birthday in March, I came home and found a huge metal tub in our living room. "Surprise!" Jeff said.

"What the hell is this?" I asked. Peering down into the tub I spied two fluffy little creatures. One was clearly a duckling. The other?

"That little duck is sick," Jeff explained. "Ed was just gonna get rid of him, so I said I'd take him." Taking a closer look, the second strange-looking creature was indeed a duck, but its poor neck was bent at an unnatural angle such that its head seemed too heavy for its body. With its head constantly upside down, walking was out of the question. On top of that oddity, poor baby duck also had an outrageous tuft of thick black downy feathers on its head.

"What are we supposed to do with it?" It was just like Jeff to bring animals home without a solid game plan. "Is it gonna die?"

"I don't know! I just wanted its last days to be pleasant."

"Well what about the other one?"

"I wanted him to have a friend." It was sweet. And also smelly and messy and a big pain in my ass. But I couldn't argue with where his heart was. That poor deformed baby could barely eat or drink. He just sat huddled up with his buddy, drawing comfort.

I hit Google hard. Upside-down duckling head. Weak-neck duckling. Broken-looking-neck duckling. After a bit of exploring, I hit pay dirt. "Babe," I yelled from the living room. Jeff popped his head in from outside.

"What?"

"It's just a vitamin E deficiency! We can put it in its water."

"Are you serious?" And with that, he was off to the drugstore.

Within a week, our sweet broken duck had a name—Norman, after his crazy hair that reminded Gus of the movie *ParaNorman*—and a tall straight neck. He could move around and eat and drink. It was a huge win for us. Life was precious. We had saved this little guy.

Jeff left for Georgia, and the ducks grew bigger and no longer fit in the container he'd brought them home in. So my beautiful new claw-foot tub became their home. Gus would invite friends over to see them swim in the tub and feed them treats. Every single day I'd have to clean out their shavings and endless duck poop. It was hard not to see it as a metaphor: make something beautiful for the baby you thought you were gonna have and then watch it get shit all over. But, for what it was worth, I loved the ducks. Gus and I held them and stroked their glossy feathers.

Alice gave birth in April, a couple of days before Jeff's birthday. Ed had told us that she would wander off on her own when she was ready. So one sunny Saturday when we didn't see her out in the back pasture, we raced with Gus along the fence line until we found her. She rocked her body against the fence, scratching her butt and bearing down. We stood a distance off, not wanting to interfere with her process. And then very quickly, without a sound, a huge sac dropped from her and Gus's eyes went wide.

"What's THAT?!?"

"That's the baby, dude." Alice went to work, licking at the embryonic sac until her soggy, red-haired baby emerged. We stayed there, the three of us, for a long time. We stayed while Alice groomed her baby. We stayed as the baby slowly climbed up onto its rickety new legs. We stayed until we got a good look and declared, "It's a boy!"

"What are we naming him, Gus?"

There was no hesitation: "Alexander!"

It was springtime on Mischief Farm. Babies were everywhere. Baby chicks at the feed store. Baby dairy cows in the field. Baby bunnies and foxes in our woods. But the things I used to delight in now served as a reminder of how broken I felt. Jeff was home, but I was avoiding him. We didn't know how to talk to each other. The things I needed to hear, he didn't know how to say; and the things he needed me to be, I couldn't be. We moved around the same spaces, but not together. He wouldn't enter a room until I left it. I wouldn't tell him where I was going; I'd just leave and hide out in the garden or in town. I was just a vessel, and I was empty. Any energy I did have was going to Gus; I had nothing left for Jeff.

I took a job filming a movie for a few weeks out of town. I needed that. With Gus at my side, we drove north across the Canadian border to Montreal, where we didn't think about the farm or babies. We practiced our French and went to museums and shows and relished being pedestrians. For three whole weeks, we were city people. Jeff was down in Georgia working. We couldn't have been farther apart.

Coming home in May, I hit the ground running. I couldn't feel anything if I kept busy, so I became the most task-oriented person in town. The garden I planted at Samuel's was overflowing with blooms. Gus's class snacks were lavish Pinterest-worthy creations. My garden was incredibly tidy. All the little sprouts of weeds were targets for my suppressed emotions. Kill kill kill.

I worried Jeffrey. I knew that I was a shell of myself. I knew that he could see it. So I avoided him.

He found me down in the garden one day. I had collected a heap of rocks that were left over from a landscaping project. Pulling them out, one by one from the back of the Rhino, I was laying a path through our large vegetable garden that would allow me easier access to our snap peas, beans, tomatoes, and cucumbers at the back of the garden. I'd pinched my hand between two large stones and blood caked my knuckles.

"Talk to me," he said, hands shoved down deep in his pockets.

"What are you talking about? I'm fine." I was angry. I'd wanted to talk months before. I'd wanted him to hold me in bed while I cried. I'd wanted him to not have been so difficult about getting pregnant in the first place. I'd wanted him to not disappear to go chop wood and then get resentful that I was doing the exact same thing. What's good for the goose, right? I'd wanted him to know I was angry and then apologize. And these mantras of anger had been running in my head for months. But then—

"I'm sorry," he said.

Jeffrey had finally seen me. We talked about our grief. We talked about how we both felt like failures. We talked about how lonely we were. Suddenly, standing there with his hands in his pockets, Jeffrey was a different person. He was incredibly vulnerable. He talked to me about how much he valued me and that this was home and that it was worth any fight.

And as we talked, he started helping me. He stood and went to get a whole bunch of rocks, laying pathways through the garden for me. Each path was a manifestation of what he was saying. We worked on this garden together.

Uncertainty still rattled around in my brain. *I don't know. I don't know. I don't know.* I didn't know how long this transformation would last. I worried that Jeff was home for only two days at a time. I wondered whether this peace was going to continue past this visit. Would he grow frustrated with me for being depressed? (I can say now I was absolutely depressed; I simply didn't realize it at the time.) But, in the end, I knew this family and this farm and this life together were worth the fight.

We began working in tandem. It was warm enough that the ducks were ready to be moved outside. But they needed a proper house to keep them safe at night. So Jeff used scraps of lumber and some old galvanized metal to build them the ultimate duck hut. We set it up together by the chicken houses.

When I was a kid, Dad told me a story about how my grandmother Dorothy had a pet duck that followed her around everywhere in the house. I never understood the appeal of having a duck as a pet until we moved to Mischief Farm. Ducks are weird. They're so expressive. They chase and kill mice; they terrify the dogs; they go down with the Highland cattle and get in the cows' feed; they have zero fear.

I wanted to be a duck.

One morning that spring I was planting flowers around the trees in front of the shop when I struck up a conversation with a regular customer named David. He sat on the bench while I dug around the roots of the trees to fit in mums and lantana. "You gotta come by Astor sometime," he said.

"What's Astor?"

"That big brick building around the corner. The one with the gates."

I had always slowed down as I drove past the big Renaissance-style Astor Home for Children building. At Halloween, dozens of lit-up jack-o-lanterns lined its stone wall. But no one ever talked about what went on there.

"What's the story?" I asked.

"I work with the kids there," David explained. "I just see all the stuff you've done here at Samuel's. The dorms there are bad. Like, really bad. You should do over there what you've done here."

Coincidentally, a couple of weeks later, Tara came to me and asked whether she and some other women could use Samuel's as a meeting space as they discussed Astor.

"Totally cool," I said. "In fact, a guy who volunteers over there has been telling me about it. Can I introduce you guys?"

There had been rumors about the Astor building, built in 1914 by Vincent Astor to house the Astor Home for Children. False rumors, mind you. We'd lived in town for five years and never realized that the "scary place for the criminally insane" we'd heard about was that brick behemoth around the corner. Legend had it that once it had been taken over by Catholic Charities in the 1940s, it had been run by nuns who tried to separate the kids who lived there from the rest of town, and everyone in town still spoke of it in hushed tones.

I was just supposed to provide introductions, but Tara showed up with Kate Kortbus, a powerhouse New Yorker who makes things happen, and her best friend, Lawrie Firestone, who is literally walking sunshine. It didn't take much persuading to get me to sit down with the group.

I learned a lot. Astor Services for Children and Families isn't an institution; it's a salve. The people there treat and care for the victims of the very worst child abuse in the state. It's a residential treatment center, and usually about sixty kids are living there at any given time. The amazing staff provide quality education and mental health services for children with behavioral and emotional health problems and for children at risk of placement in foster care, and they offer help to families that need assistance in developing the skills necessary to raise their children in challenging environments.

Lawrie told me how badly the group needed money, especially to renovate the dorms. As they talked about these kids, and about specific horror stories they had lived through, I began to take it very personally. I wanted another child desperately. I had all this aching room left in my heart for a child. How could other people hurt their kids?

Telling Stories

The Burtons are liars. My father chief among us. When we were little, he told us he met my mother saving her from a dragon and that he kept the dragon's head locked away in the mysterious black trunk out in the shed. My mother would solemnly nod and casually throw in key details—the angry giant, the white horse, her gown. In reality, Dad met Mom when she was nineteen and a checkout girl at the Giant supermarket. He was thirty-two and sure of himself, and it wasn't a white horse, but a white Monte Carlo with a flashy burgundy interior. So, perhaps the story was true after all.

Once, Johnny Zarling, our neighbor and our pastor's youngest son, asked why Dad had lost his hair. Wild Bill took the opportunity to beef up his legendary status, telling us it had been ripped out while he and his Green Beret buddies were rescuing a pack of kidnapped children from a monster called The Claw that lived on top of the water tower a couple blocks away. When we asked why a cop car was parked at Gramma's house, he told us she was an undercover detective. I believed that one till I was sixteen and my parents overheard me telling a friend about my badass Gramma. They burst out laughing. Turns out, my aunt was just having a *thing* with a police officer.

The trait is definitely hereditary. I'm a liar, too. For the first few months we were together, Jeffrey thought I was thirty years old. The night I met him, I figured I'd never see him again, so I rounded up from twenty-six. And then I promptly forgot about it, until we were celebrating my birthday. My best friend, Nick, hoisted his glass in the air and toasted, "Twenty-seven club!" Jeff demanded to see my driver's license.

Gus is my latest victim. He believes that there's a door to the fairy Kingdom on Mischief Farm. *There is indeed a tree with a doorknob and a Knocker.* When he turns eighteen he'll be able to tap in to his magical abilities and step through the portal. Or, he'll just become a liar like the rest of us.

Clearly, narrative, true or not, is of the utmost importance to us Burtons. We were never the best-looking or the wealthiest Kids. We didn't have the advantages we saw other Kids enjoy. But we could weave a helluva story. And we could turn misfortune into a great tale, which has turned out to be a gift that has saved my life.

Tara suggested that we take a look at the building, so we walked up the street to the beautiful structure, with its gorgeous hand-carved details in the stone above the solid wooden doors that look like something you'd find on a castle. But inside we found a nightmare. We're talking Oliver Twist–level bad. Nothing had been updated since the 1950s, and the kids' dorms were cold and sterile, like prison cellblocks. We were greeted by Sonia Barnes-Moorhead, who was clearly in charge. She was warm and very up front about the facility's need for help.

Suddenly, when I needed it most, here was another sign from the universe. I'd been grieving for six months and ruining my life. My grief was making me someone I hated. It was ruining my relationship with Jeffrey. It was ruining my ability to be a good mother. So, right there, I pivoted.

I said to myself, *Okay, well I'm not having any more kids, but I still have all this energy to put into kids. I like them. I like good kids. I like naughty kids. I like being around them. I like their chaos.*

So all this energy for children that I had, I poured into Astor. The group met again at Samuel's. "We're going to throw a fund-raising event this fall that will pay for the materials for a renovation," I told them. "Some paint and some creature comforts will go a long way in fixing the place up. Let's do a show."

"A show?" Tara asked. She was my theater junkie friend. "Like a play?"

"No, more like a vaudeville bit. Short acts. Like storytelling." My wheels were spinning. "What if we did an evening of ghost stories? That was the best part of being a kid—sitting around trying to scare each other."

"I like that!" Kate-the-powerhouse said.

"Think we can get everything ready by October?"

"Honey," Kate said, "we can do anything."

When it was time for Jeff to leave again to go to Georgia, he asked me to go with him. The building of the house addition had dragged on and on, and without the baby to fill the spare room, I just wanted it over and done with. I asked the contractors whether they'd be able to work faster if we weren't in their way.

"Absolutely," they said.

So we loaded up my truck, and the whole family made our way down to the heat of Georgia for the summer. Before I could cultivate any more flowerbeds or raise any more new animals, we needed to work on the core of the farm—the three of us. Ed found people to watch over the animals while we were gone. Gus and I enjoyed an easy summer of waiting for Dad to come home from work, working on the Ghost Stories event for the fall, cooking, going on rambles in the woods, playing in creeks, and diving into all-around laziness.

Gus and I also popped over for a short trip to Wilmington, North Carolina, to visit my parents for my dad's birthday. A couple of my brothers were around as well, and as we settled in one night, Gus started talking about boats and how cool they were. My brother Billy, who was in from LA, said, "Hold up dude. You'll like this."

Next thing I know, *Titanic* was on. I hadn't seen that movie since it came out in theaters, and it was *the* movie you went to see on dates. I had never been a big fan, but then I heard a voice that I loved. Bill Paxton, with his glorious 1990s earring and naughty grin, opened the movie, and Gus started yelling, "Mr. Bill! Mr. Bill! That's Uncle Bill!"

Gus was beaming. Transfixed. I texted Bill:

> I'm watching *Titanic* with Gus for the first time and he's fucking
> obsessed. You're the coolest person in his book right now.

Gus watched the movie every day from then on. We fast-forwarded through the sexy parts; then he wanted to watch it three times a day forever, so at some point I thought, dammit, if Jack and Rose are his first window into romance, that's fine. I hope he lives up to that standard; he'll like brassy chicks.

A week later when we got back to Jeff's house in Georgia, a package was waiting for us from Bill. While he had prepared for the role, he had gone down in a submarine to tour the *Titanic* wreck. He had kept a journal and written entries and drawn beautiful, intricate pictures; and when he came back, he printed up a few copies for his dear friends. He sent one to Gus, and the kid walked around telling everyone, "I'm friends with the guy who found the *Titanic*."

It was the end of summer, and school beckoned. Jeff had to continue working in Georgia, so I loaded up Gus and the dogs (we'd picked up a puppy—Honey—in a Waffle House parking lot) and made a pit stop at my folks' house on the way back to New York. My dad offered to make the drive with me so we could take up a trailer of furniture for the addition, which was supposed to be near completion.

Dad and I drove all day, and I taught him how to cyber-stalk people on Facebook, which led to hours of fun looking up all his buddies from childhood and the army. At the end of a twelve-hour drive, we rolled up to our home—to see house wrap flapping around in the dark. Making our way up to the front porch, there were no lights, and a path of plywood is all that covered the exposed beams of the porch. Inside, a dirty paint roller was dried to my kitchen sink, and there was no toilet paper to be found anywhere in the house.

"What the hell is going on here?" my dad asked—the same question in my mind. We were so exhausted that I just wanted to put Gus to bed.

The next morning, my dad got to work. He'd been a quality-assurance inspector for years, so his job was to go to work sites and assess what was being done wrong. Not only was our addition not finished, but some of what had been built was done so incorrectly it required demo before it could be fixed. I was devastated. The physical expression of our plan to grow our family had totally gone to shit.

My dad started making calls to builders. I may have been a grown-ass woman with a child, but it was still reassuring that my father jumped in to help me set things right, or at least fire off a warning shot to scare off the coyotes. When I was working on *One Tree Hill* my dad came to work with his bullwhip on a day I was shooting a scene with a shitty, pervy boss. When we broke for lunch, I found Dad showing off his bullwhip tricks in the parking lot with our sound mixer, Mike, who had once worked for the circus. They were hooting and hollering while cracking the leather hard enough that the creep could hear it in his office.

Dad found someone to give us a second opinion on the work that had been done. Mark McEathron was a builder whose kids went to school with Gus. Through mutual friends I had heard he was a stand-up guy—and he passed my father's knowledge test, so things were looking up. Our candy store electricians, the Stanhopes, showed up. Ed recommended a few guys to help with odd jobs.

The list of things that needed to be accomplished was endless. Jeff was frustrated that he wasn't there, but we'd been working hard at communicating and learning to be at ease together again, so I wanted to fix this house to prove to him that we could fix anything. Thankfully, the new team my dad assembled turned the whole thing around.

I did any job I had the skill set to do, which meant that I painted *everything*—the blades of the ceiling fan, the shiplap for the bedroom and bathroom. The biggest bear was the garage. We wanted to paint it the same color as the house, so in the late heat of September, my dad and I rolled and painted the entirety of the huge building with primer and then three coats of paint. (Fun fact: When you live on a hill where the wind is blowing all day long, you don't get to take advantage of the ease of a spray gun. No one tells you that when you buy the house on a hill.)

As we painted, I bounced ideas off my dad for the Astor Ghost Stories event, which I'd foolishly imagined I'd be quietly working on while sitting in our new addition. It was slated for October at the Fisher Center at Bard College; Jeffrey and I would read ghost stories, along with our friends Griffin Dunne and Mary Stuart Masterson, who I was quickly learning is a force of nature up here. Kate and Lawrie and Sonia and Tara and all the other folks involved with Astor had done a wonderful job of getting the technical stuff together, but it was my job to bring the show. It *had* to be good. This was the first time anyone in town was really talking about Astor. We were introducing this institution to our community even though it had been there for sixty years.

Jeff wanted to visit Astor and spend time with the kids before the event. He can be awkward around adults, but kids are his wheel-house, and he went to hang out with them in their English class.

I had been pulling stories for Jeff, Mary, and Griffin to read—Ray Bradbury, Edward Gorey, Edgar Allan Poe. A literature junkie, I was excited about bringing stories alive that I'd loved my whole life. But Jeffrey wasn't as enthusiastic. That idea lacked originality to him, and if he's anything, he's original. So, after holding court with a group of kids, he said out of the blue, "Hey, I want each of you to write a ghost story, and I'm going to read your stories at this performance." Needless to say, they freaked out. Negan from *The Walking Dead* was gonna read their stories in front of hundreds of people?! Their teacher was such a good sport.

We had no idea whether his idea would work. What if the stories were scattered or confusing or too sad? There were so many vari-ables when working with these very special students. But Jeffrey never doubted his plan. "It's gonna be awesome," he assured me.

The day of the performance I had been at the theater all day doing sound check, programming the lighting cues and the sound cues and other last-minute stuff. The venue is used largely for sympho-nies or operas or very meticulous productions. I hadn't done a cue sheet for anything since my theater days in high school! I just kept telling the lighting designer, "Jeff will probably walk around a lot, so just keep a light on him."

"But will he be standing or sitting?"

"I'm not sure."

"Will you guys share a mic or need your own?"

The Fisher Center was lovely about dealing with my brand of crazy, but I was completely overwhelmed. An hour before the show

Jeffrey showed up, decked out in a brand-new suit. This is not a man who likes to dress up. I think the last time he'd put a suit on was during our courtship in New Mexico when he'd donned a black suit and black shirt, turning himself into my own personal Johnny Cash. And here he was seven years later, looking beautiful in a soft, light-gray suit with a turtleneck. It was so un-farmy. He had gotten all cleaned up and came out guns blazing. I'd been killing myself on this event. And with that simple romantic effort, he showed me he was really there for me.

The kids from Astor sat in the back of the auditorium and watched Negan perform their stories and get huge laughs from the audience. Seven hundred people were clapping for them. After, I received letters from their mothers that told me how that tiny thing had transformed their kids.

Jeff started doing a lot of press with me to promote Astor. When he's on set or at a convention, he's around big groups of people, and everybody wants a piece of him. He's incredibly generous with himself. So when he's home, that's his time to recuperate. Watching him use his reserves to promote Astor made me fall in love with him all over. He knew it was important to me, so it became important to him.

Jeffrey had shown up, and I knew that meant we were going to push through the shitty stuff together and keep going. From that moment on, we were stronger than we'd ever been. In working for others, we found ourselves again.

15

I want to feel all there is to feel, he thought. Let
me feel tired, now, let me feel tired. I mustn't
forget, I'm alive, I know I'm alive, I mustn't forget
it tonight or tomorrow or the day after that.

—Ray Bradbury, *Dandelion Wine*

After Ghost Stories in October, I let my guard down. I had given up on getting pregnant. Or that's what I said. It always existed as a nagging desire in the back of my mind. We were missing a family member. I felt it in my bones.

In December, Jeff got a job that would take him to New Zealand, and Gus and I were going along. Before we left, I had a feeling that I was pregnant. I've always had really low levels of hormones, so any time my body starts doing something, I know right away. My boobs hurt, and I was nauseated. I tried to keep my heart in lock-down. Having lost one pregnancy, I was gun-shy about making declarations ever again. I didn't celebrate. I didn't go to the doctor. I didn't tell anyone other than Jeff, and he also was very hesitant to get excited.

Jeff was playing King Arthur for a commercial, so he was off wearing armor all day while Gus and I toured New Zealand. The place stole our hearts. The people were so kind, and the whole country felt like Mischief Farm—rolling green hills and ponds. Highland cattle and sheep. Maybe we could just move there and do Peter Jackson movies.

Then, one afternoon Gus and I took a walk, and I felt a sharp pain. I thought, *Oh, I know what's going on here. I've been down this road before.* I could feel my hormones doing all sorts of weird shit. It was another miscarriage. But it had been so early in the pregnancy, and I'd tried so hard to tame my emotions, keep myself from feeling joy or relief, that the loss didn't cut me in the same way that the first one had. And we were having wonderful family time, and that helped to ease the loss. I thought to myself, I'm well-practiced now. How many times can this happen to me? Am I going to get better with this each time? That was a shitty concept.

Jeff said, "We're just going to keep trying, Hil."

We did keep trying, and about six weeks later, in January, I got pregnant again. This time I went to the doctor and got ultrasounds. There was a heartbeat.

I had been working on *Lethal Weapon*, and while we were in New Zealand the producers asked me to come back. The executive producer and creator of the show, Matt Miller, had been my boss on *Forever*, and I liked working with him. He had always been fair with me and very kind. When I had trouble finding child care, he found a babysitter in the city. For this new show, he had created the role and flat out offered it to me. But, as much as I loved to work, the offer was the standard base rate—the kind of money you make as a first-time actor.

"You guys aren't even paying me enough to cover child care and expenses," I told him, "and I'm doing all the work the boys are doing, but not making near as much money. I want to do it, but I can't afford to do it." Matt personally went to bat with Warner Bros. and got me more money than I'd asked for. I respect the hell out of him.

I didn't want to tell anyone about the pregnancy and jinx myself the way I'd done before, but it would have been irresponsible to not tell Matt. I felt awful throwing him a curveball—"Hey, I'm pregnant. I'm really sorry, but I can't do stunts." Then, I had to tell the stunt coordinator, "Hey, I'm pregnant, so let's be careful." They graciously hired a stunt double for me so I wouldn't have to do anything compromising, and they scheduled me so that I'd have ample rest between my scenes. That production couldn't have been sweeter.

Early in pregnancy, doctors test your hormone levels to see whether they have doubled. My levels were very low, but they had doubled. So I was optimistic but also cautious. With Gus back in New York with Jeffrey, I sat around in my hotel room, not moving a muscle, and finally reading the books my sister-in-law Jess had given me when I had lost the first baby. Learning about the divine feminine and the life of Mary Magdalene blew my mind. I read about the Black Madonna statues in Europe, which are said to possess great power. I was gonna read and read until I was a wise earth mama, a witchy woman in caftans who cured ailments with herbs and faith.

Then I woke up in the hotel early one morning, and everything was gone.

I called Jeff. The distance between who we had been the first time we miscarried versus who we were now helped tremendously. I had my partner back. He said the things I needed to hear. We'd lost again. But we'd also won somehow in the midst of that.

I went to my brother Billy's house and spent the day with him, which was a good distraction. And my best friend from sixth grade, Erica, happened to be in Los Angeles for work, so we had a slumber party and I pretended that I was eleven again.

The next day I had to go to work and tell everyone who had been so lovely and so accommodating that I had lost the baby. They were kind. Members of the crew had just heard the trickle-down good news that I was expecting, and as they congratulated me, I had to admit that I had just miscarried. Clayne Crawford, the male lead of the show, was between setups. We had a short scene outside with a car stunt—my character was casually supposed to hit a bad guy who was trying to escape. Clayne walked up to me and asked, "How we feeling mama?" He's a dad. His wife Kiki and I had become good friends. I just shook my head, and he knew. He pulled me into a hug. "I'm so sorry."

I had to tell Matt. That sweet man had bent over backwards tailoring this role to fit to Gus's school schedule and my availability and then my pregnancy and now this. "Okay," Matt said. "Will you come back next year and work?" My character had essentially been written off the show out of respect to my and the baby's well-being.

"Yes, absolutely." He gave me a light at the end of the tunnel.

When I got home, I promised myself to be more present and to focus on what I had, rather than on what I felt I was lacking. Sharagim had given birth to a gorgeous baby girl in August, so I'd made a habit of taking her older boys, who were Gus's best friends, so she could get a night off here and there. One night, when the crowd of boys were over, making bed forts and whooping it up, I checked my phone.

Bill Paxton had died unexpectedly from complications after surgery.

Jeffrey was away at a convention. I knew he'd hear the news, and I didn't want a bunch of people watching him when he found out. I texted him.

Call me please. It's important.

Bill was a guy who lived life right. He adored his wife. He delighted in his children. He loved his industry. He spread joy with such ease. It all felt like so much to endure in so short a span of time: Ira's death, Bisou, the miscarriages, and now Bill. This had been a period of incredible loss for our family, and as I heard Jeff choke back tears, I just wanted to find a way to stop it. It was especially difficult for him. A number of his friends had passed in the previous year, and he realized that he had hit that age when people aren't getting married anymore, people aren't having babies anymore—people are having funerals. He made it home after the convention and we sat in our room. "I'm sad, ma," he said.

"I know babe. Me too." Sometimes there's nothing to do but let the tidal wave of grief hit you and wait for the next break in the waves.

There had been so much sorrow in the previous few years, but Jeffrey and I had made it through together. That spring was filled with celebration. In March we went to Barcelona where Jeffrey and his best friend, Norman Reedus, were filming an episode of Norman's show *Ride*. Jeffrey was clinging very tightly to his friendships.

While the boys filmed, Gus and I wandered the cobblestone streets of Barcelona, exploring markets and the zoo and wax museums and all the curiosities the city had to offer. I fell in love with Barcelona and was excited for Jeffrey's day off so we could all roam around together. Hand in hand in hand, we walked aimlessly, stopping to watch street performers do magic or blow huge bubbles for the kids. We stopped in every beautiful deli, jambon sandwiches calling to us from their glass cases. Turning down a windy street, we found ourselves entering a large square. Little café tables lined the block, and people casually milled about. At the end of this square was a building so remarkable, I stopped and stared. I didn't have to say anything. Jeff just knew. Before us was the Barcelona Cathedral. He'd seen that look on my face before at the Loretto Chapel in Santa Fe, a mix of awe and elation. "Come on buddy. Your mom wants to see this."

A gothic masterpiece, the church was exquisite, all ancient stonework and elaborate carvings, and the air was cool and smelled of incense. I breathed it in as Jeff, Gus, and I stood in a long line of pilgrims. When we were ushered in, we moved to the left, exploring the statues of the saints that lined the cathedral. It quickly became apparent that I was moving at a much slower pace than Jeff and Gus, so they peeled off. "Let's give Mama some space."

I wandered across the stone floors worn from hundreds of years of worship. Not growing up Catholic, I had no idea of the protocol. Do I cross myself? Kneel? I walked and walked until I reached a smiling statue. This one beamed, far different from her stoic neighbors. *Mary Magdalene*. Of course. Those books Jess had given me had provided a framework for how I felt about this woman. I'd been raised to believe that she was a woman of ill repute. But religious research disputed that, and even the Catholic Church had just given her a feast day, essentially apologizing and announcing that the Magdalene had never been a prostitute. For the first time in my life I lit a votive candle. Not for a baby necessarily. It wasn't a wishing well. I asked for the strength to be a better woman, however that manifested. I don't know how much time I spent there, but I felt moved. I cried.

Continuing along my path, I descended a small flight of stairs. A few people were milling about, looking through intricate metalwork at something in a shrine. A Black Madonna. I couldn't believe it. I knew there was one at Montserrat, an hour outside of the city. But to see one here, so unexpectedly, caught me off guard. Finally, when I got to the virgin, I was overwhelmed by the kindness of her face and the joy of her son. More than a reverent depiction, she felt like a real mother. It felt like a sign.

Years before, during the filming of *The Secret Life of Bees*, the head of the art department brought me a present. "I thought you might like this," he had said, handing me a prop jar of honey with a Black Madonna label on it. The story of the Black Madonna had been a plot point in the book and movie—female empowerment and belief in the divine feminine. I still had that jar of honey on my special shelf of first-edition books. I treasured it as a memory of my favorite work experience, surrounded by women. And here it was, manifesting in my real life so many years later. For the second time in my life, I lit a candle, sending up a prayer for grace.

Back home, spring was frisky. All the alpacas that we inherited from Sunny are boys and are gelded, with the exception of Zeus. He's a pure black alpaca, and even though he's a little guy, he's real sure of himself; he's always the first one to the trough. He's the Joe Pesci of alpacas. When I give them their monthly shots, Zeus is the one who likes to make it tough for me. He's antagonistic, and when I'm not careful, he backs me into a corner. He's not any nicer at shearing time either.

The boys' fleece goes to Sunny, who sends it off and gets it made into the softest, most beautiful yarn you've ever seen, and then she just gives it back to me saying, "Oh, well, you knit more than I do. You take this."

The first couple of years shearing the alpacas was terrifying because the shearing business around here is a cutthroat game of who you know. Shearers are booked up from early spring through summer, and if they don't know you and they don't recognize your phone number, they're not coming over. The first spring on the farm I called around and got recommendations from local farmers, but no one would return my calls. Not a single person. Once, I actually got a guy on the phone and he said he'd come out the following Thursday. He never showed. Finally, we found somebody to help us. He barely spoke. He was in a hurry. It wasn't fun.

It's all hands on deck for shearing, and the animals don't like it one bit. Alpacas, for the most part, won't spit at you the way llamas do; they're pretty hard to piss off. But boy, when they're getting sheared, it's a shower of bile. So while two guys are shearing the animal, I go through and pick up all the fiber that's being sheared before it gets a spit shower. And this spit is no normal drool; it's the nastiest, greenest vomit you've ever seen. There was no way Jeffrey and I could handle shearing on our own.

The second year, the shearer who had helped us before disappeared, and we had another bad experience finding someone. So that spring when we got a call from our contractor-hero, Mark McEathron, about some alpacas, I was intrigued but knew I needed to play hardball.

He and his wife, Jess, had an elderly neighbor who was looking to downsize her farm. "She has these award-winning beautiful alpaca girls," Mark said. "Would you guys be interested in taking them? She wants them to go to a good home."

These girls Mark was talking about were really pretty, with great pedigree, and their fiber was *fancy*. But adding more alpacas with no shearer contact in sight wasn't the smartest plan. "I'd be happy to take the girls," I told him, "but only if your neighbor shares her shearer contact with me." It was like a drug hookup.

The deal was made.

Not long after, these gentlemen drove up in a big white pickup truck with their name—Twist of Fate Spinnery—on the side of it. They were pros. The animals stayed calm. There was minimal bile. The process was fast. And not only did they shear the animals, they also had the ability to process the fleece for you so you could get it turned into felting or yarn, or you could have it washed and then spin it yourself.

So the boys got sheared, the girls got trailered in, and we gave them a pasture on the opposite end of the farm from the boys, so they wouldn't get all rowdy. You don't want your alpacas getting riled up. But I guess that pheromone must've traveled across the entire farm, because all of a sudden Zeus lost his mind. He was trying to climb fences just to get the attention of those girls. And they weren't paying him any mind. It was like watching a high school boy in love.

Jeff asked the natural questions: "What should we do now? Should we breed them? Is that our next step?"

Now, these girls are a big deal. It's like the difference between getting a mutt in a Waffle House parking lot and getting a purebred poodle that won Westminster. They are supermodel alpacas, with beautiful straight teeth and perfect fiber. Our boys all have crooked teeth and knobby knees, so when I figure out how to get them together, it will be like *Freaks and Geeks.*

I can envision Zeus hanging out with the girls and then coming back to the other guys, like, "You guys have no idea what you're missing."

Spring also meant it was time to put my money where my mouth was when it came to the renovation of the Astor building. Our fundraiser had been successful, and we now had the money needed to start tackling the first wing of the residential center. Kate and Lawrie and Sonia were all systems go. I'd certainly completed my fair share of home improvement projects over the years, but this was different. If you fuck up at home, no biggie. At a clinical children's home? Big problem. Huge. I knew I needed a professional skill set to pull this off.

Remember how heartbroken and hurt I was when I came home

and found the addition in shambles? It would appear that everything really does happen for a reason. To my absolute delight, Mark and his crew, the Stanhopes, our new plumber, Tim, and a buddy of Ed's named Frank all volunteered to help with the difficult task of renovating an entire wing of Astor in five short days. We could work on the space only while the kids were in school, so coordinating all the volunteers and doing the labor in a timely fashion was a monumental task. Mark took a tour through the unit and called in a master painter friend, Mike Diblasi. Mike is a quiet guy, and he looked around the space seriously. "Oh no," I thought. There were huge cracks in the wall and chunks of plaster falling down around the doorways. "He's gonna tell me this is not doable."

But instead, he put his hands on his hips and said, "Yeah, I know a material that can smooth all this out."

Had the original addition plans at the farm worked out, I never would have met most of these guys. It was inspiring to have all these craftsmen who'd helped us at the farm give up paychecks for an entire week because they saw the same thing I saw—a place devoid of hope and childhood liveliness—and they wanted to help fix it.

Kate had called for a meeting, and I presented the design plan to the group. I turned photos I had of the space into black and white and then printed them out and painted over them—the same way I'd worked on the color scheme for Samuel's. It was amateur, but it got the idea across. The first unit was all boys, so I wanted to do a camping theme. To me, it was frustrating that these kids had been moved to the Hudson Valley, a place renowned for its beautiful outdoors, and they were stuck inside this building. Bringing the outside in made sense. With sky blues and greens,

I added tree decals to the design, wanting to create a forest for them to daydream in. All the rugs and pillows and art added to the scene. When I presented the design to the group, I expected clinical feedback or pushback on what was allowed in the space. With the exception of my curtain suggestions, which James the building manager informed me weren't up to fire code, the plan was met with excitement.

Phase one of fundraising had gone well. Phase two of designing was approved. Now we just had to do the renovation!

I'd drop Gus off at school and then race around town like a madwoman, securing supplies or trying to get donations. The wonderful folks at Davis Furniture in Poughkeepsie had been so nice when I was looking for dressers for the new addition at our house. I sheepishly went back and asked, "Could you maybe spare a desk or chair from your back discount room?" To which they said, "No, no, no," and pulled out all their furniture catalogues for me to pick out something brand new for the space. It was incredibly generous. Williams Lumber had been my and Jeff's go-to for everything since we had moved to the area. Sharagim's husband, Sean, introduced me to one of the owners, Kim Williams. "We're doing this project over at Astor . . ." I didn't even need to finish the sentence.

"Whatever you need," she responded. Then, going the extra mile, she referred me to Rob Hunter, the local Benjamin Moore rep. All of a sudden we were getting all of our paint donated! Samuel's sent over coffee, and one of my favorite crystal shops offered to do chakra cleansing for the staff and volunteers. Friends picked Gus up at school so I could stay later with James and get more done. Our community rallied and connected over this heartfelt effort to improve the lives of these kids.

Mike Diblasi single-handedly rebuilt and painted all the walls in that wing, carrying around a tray of heavy cementlike compound as if it were nothing. Mark and his team created shelving for every bedroom so each kid could put together a little shrine of their prized possessions. They built benches for the dining room and replaced all the molding in the unit, sanding down all the edges to make everything safe. Tim, the plumber, tore out and redid the rundown kitchen and repaired the bathrooms. The Stanhopes came in early in the week and replaced every lighting fixture with bright new LED units that transformed the space. And then they returned every day after to help with odd jobs like decals and painting trim.

Each night I wrote a note to the kids. I figured it must be odd for them to have strangers in their space making a mess and moving everything around. I hoped it wasn't traumatic for them.

Late in the week, while the army of moms, led by Kate and Lawrie, made beds and treated each child's bedroom as if it were their own kid's, I talked with Sonia. "I'm not sure the crew should stay for the reveal with the kids," Sonia said, gently. "Some of them have a lot of emotional walls up. I'd hate for any of them to have a bad reaction and the crew to not understand."

"I totally get it," I said. I knew some of these children were nonverbal. It wouldn't be like those makeover shows on TV. The chances of someone being upset by the change were high.

So we had a private reveal on Friday, with our entire crew and our donors and members of the press. Astor had been shrouded in secrecy for so long, it was important that we spread the word about the good work being done there.

The space looked amazing—with animals and inspirational sayings covering the walls. With Mark's wife, Jess, the local artist Tom Cale had painted a fabulous mural in the living room. The unit shined with the love that had been put into it.

Everyone hugged and shed a few tears. I thanked them after the cameras left. "For those of you who don't know, I got involved with Astor because I'd had a miscarriage, and it left a big gaping hole. Working on this with all of you has meant so much to me personally." I was having trouble getting the words out. But I wanted them to know. They didn't just fix this space for the children. They'd done me a great service as well. From the guys who worked on my house to Lawrie and Kate and the staff, I'd made a whole new circle of friends. Good people.

After everyone left, I stayed and wrote notes for each of the kids who lived on the unit. For each bedroom, we asked them about their favorite colors, favorite sports teams, favorite cartoons. Gus had helped me pick out rugs and sheets and pillows and stuffed animals. I was nervous as I waited for the kids to come up. James and Sonia waited with me. Then suddenly, from the staircase in the hallway, I heard whooping and laughter and little boys shouting. "Oh man!" "Lookit, lookit!"

I peered around the corner, and the group of boys who lived in the unit were darting from room to room. They were bursting with excitement like it was Christmas morning. Sonia and James and I all looked at each other. We hadn't been expecting that. One by one, the boys came up with pillows or toys they'd found on their beds. "Is this really mine?"

"That's all yours, dude." And then they wrapped me in hugs. They pulled me down to hang out in the living room on the camping-themed carpet we'd put in. It was a dog pile of affection. I cried the whole way home.

Jeff made it back home for a short weekend toward the end of May. He'd been tapped to drive the pace car for the Indy 500, so we were going to make a family adventure out of it. I have a picture of Gus greeting him when he got home that day. We were all so happy to see each other.

In the midst of all our busy-ness, we had another project up our sleeves. The year before had been a test for our relationship. I had been the worst version of myself. Jeffrey had been distant and unreachable. And yet somehow we had found each other again, and we wanted to seal the deal.

We had called each other "husband" and "wife" throughout everything. But we had never actually gotten around to getting married. In the English language there is not a word for what we are. I've always felt like "fiancé" is a pretentious word. I most certainly wasn't gonna call him my boyfriend. "Baby Daddy" felt like I was trying too hard. He wasn't my husband, but the title would have to do. We did all the legal stuff. We were each other's next-of-kin. We could pull the plug on each other. (That's romantic, huh?) We owned property together. We owned businesses together. We owned homes together. We had a child together. We'd literally done everything together except have a wedding. I kept saying let's just go to the courthouse, but Jeffrey is a romantic person, so we planned a wedding—a destination wedding on St. Maarten in the Caribbean.

We planned the whole thing that weekend. I found a dress. We picked flower arrangements and food. We invited a very small circle of friends who all RSVP'd yes and booked their villas at a beautiful resort on St. Maarten for January the next year. We put down a deposit. We were getting married!

A few days later I was at a dinner for Lawrie's birthday. I had a glass of wine and thought, this doesn't feel good. The next day I took a pregnancy test. It was June 4, 2017, and I was pregnant again. I wasn't going to tell anybody. I didn't even go to the doctor. But I sent Jeff a picture of the positive test.

"Okay," he responded. "Let's see what happens."

He felt that after I'd gotten pregnant before and he'd told me how badly he wanted a baby that he had jinxed it. So, we'd developed a weird report:

I'd say: "I'm pregnant."

He'd say: "Oh, babe, you're so pretty. Let's see what happens." And then he'd change the subject. It was like he was afraid to put any pressure on me. I could appreciate his sensitivity.

For Father's Day in June, I got Jeff three mini-donkeys. He had wanted donkeys forever, and I like to tease him about being an ass man. There was a pregnant mother donkey who was due in a couple of weeks, a yearling named Princess, and the mother's best friend, Ally. The donkeys' owner wouldn't sell me the mother without selling me her best friend too. So the three donkeys showed up.

A week later, the mama donkey gave birth. We watched as the big-eyed baby with a fuzzy Mohawk of hair teetered around, taking his first steps. He was enormously cute, and we wanted him and Mama to have some quiet time together away from Princess and Ally. We waited till he seemed steady on his legs, and then we carefully harnessed his mother and walked the two of them over to the barn, where a fresh bed of hay was waiting for them. We stood in the barn, leaning on each other and watching Mama and her baby for a good long while. *This is why we moved here.* The foal was stumbling around on new legs. When he started to nurse, Jeff took my hand and we walked back up the driveway talking about what to name him.

"What about Paxton?" I asked.

He turned and smiled, "I was just thinking that."

I laughed, "Bill would have the biggest chuckle about us naming an ass after him."

When we visit the donkeys, they're like big dogs, bursting with affection. They're such lovers. It's like a Puppy Bowl, with the animals piling on top of each other, only the animals weigh 150 to 180 pounds and have hooves and teeth. But they still want to crawl all over us and have their heads and bellies scratched.

Paxton and Jeff have a very deep bond. They are wild about each other, and Paxton is obsessed with Jeffrey. He can hear his voice from across the farm, and he'll come running up to the fence. A couple of weeks after Paxton was born we were swimming, and I saw a huge, god-awful black bruise on Jeff's ribs. "Jeffrey, what happened?!"

"Uuuhh, Paxton bit me. He wanted a kiss, and I was petting one of the other donkeys."

Gus finished up school for the year and then we went off to Los Angeles, where I was shooting another season of *Lethal Weapon.*

Cooking for Martha Stewart

While I was pregnant with George, *Allrecipes* magazine asked me to do a presentation.

I said, "Okay."

A few days later they called back: "Oh, by the way, it's going to be a cook-off with another person."

I said, "Okay."

They called again: "Oh, by the way, we need you to do a recipe that's totally your own."

I said, "Okay."

They called yet again: "Oh, by the way, the other person is going to be Dorinda Medley, of *Real Housewives*. Famous for her elaborate dinner parties."

And I still said, "Okay." But now I was nervous.

So my mother came and we hit the local farm stands and bought in-season local ingredients. Adding in my own eggs and jalapeños and blueberries from the garden, we laid everything out before us and brainstormed.

Allrecipes reached out one more time.

"Guess who's going to be judging? Martha!"

Say what? Martha Friggen Stewart would be judging the contest. (Side note: I was the teen who did not subscribe to *Vogue* or *Cosmo*, I had *Martha Stewart Living* delivered to my college dorm.)

Martha Stewart was everything I dreamed she would be. Immaculate, formidable, and gorgeous. I swallowed any pride I had and asked for a photo with her. Dorinda made me do it.

Sweet Hot Corn Cake

FOR THE SYRUP

1 cup blackberries

¼ cup honey

½ cup fresh-squeezed orange juice (I used a tangelo)

2 tablespoons orange juice

1 teaspoon cornstarch

FOR THE CORN CAKE

1 cup all-purpose flour

½ cup yellow cornmeal

¼ cup sugar

1 teaspoon baking powder

½ teaspoon baking soda

½ teaspoon salt

1¼ cups buttermilk

3 tablespoons honey

2 large eggs

3 tablespoons unsalted butter, melted and cooled

1 ear fresh corn, kernels sliced off and cob milked
(to milk the corn, after you slice off the kernels, run the blunt edge of your knife down cob and reserve any leftover pulp and liquid)

2 jalapeños, seeds and ribs removed, chopped

½ cup blackberries

Zest of 1 orange

1 teaspoon fresh thyme

Butter for frying

(continued)

Start the syrup first. In a saucepan, combine blackberries, honey, and orange juice. Bring to a boil and then reduce heat to a simmer. Let simmer so the berries cook down for 10 minutes while you prepare the corn cake.

In a large bowl, combine the dry ingredients—flour, cornmeal, sugar, baking powder, baking soda, and salt. In a separate bowl, mix your wet ingredients—buttermilk, honey, eggs, melted butter, corn, corn milk, orange zest, thyme, and jalapeños.

Combine wet and dry ingredients.

Slice blackberries into small chunks, removing any thick cores if needed. Gently fold blackberries into cornmeal batter.

Pour blackberry syrup mixture through a fine-mesh strainer. In a small bowl, combine 2 tablespoons orange juice with cornstarch. Combine well. Add small amounts of blackberry liquid to cornstarch mixture to bring the temperature up. Then add it all to the remaining blackberry liquid in a saucepan. Bring the mixture back up to a boil to thicken. Remove from heat; let cool.

Melt some butter in a nonstick skillet over medium heat. For each corn cake, add ¼ cup batter to skillet and cook until golden brown on each side.

Plate warm corn cake and top with a tab of butter. Drizzle with blackberry syrup, serve, and ENJOY!

They had an awesome storyline written for me, and I was going to be doing all these cool stunts, but now I had to sit down with sweet Matt Miller and do the whole pregnancy song and dance again.

"Do you remember that yearlong plan you had for me?" I asked him. "Well, I'm about to fuck it up again. I'm so sorry."

But Matt and his team couldn't have been more gracious. The stunt team got an amazing body double who made me look like I was in really good shape, and she did all the heavy lifting for me. Clayne Crawford took incredible care of me. All these people had been working with me on the day I had miscarried, so they knew what it meant for me to be pregnant again and were very gentle with me.

After I'd started showing, I went to the doctor fully prepared for her to give me some kind of awful news. I white-knuckled my way through my regular ultrasound, and the doctor said, "Hey, kid, everything looks good. The heartbeat is really strong and you're in your second trimester." I was amazed.

Then, she added, "But, you're over thirty-five now, so you've got to go to the high-risk doctor in Poughkeepsie."

I was afraid for that appointment, and I'd learned my lesson, so I waited for Jeff to come home to join me. I knew that when things went badly and we were separated physically, everything was worse. This time, I wanted him with me if there was bad news. When advanced paternal age is added to advanced maternal age, the probability of frightening things occurring is higher. I had asked worst-case-scenario questions during my first trip to the doctor, and she had prepped me for bad news. All I could think was that Jeff was right: we had our perfect boy, and I should call it a day. But I had wanted this baby so badly for so long.

I was edgy on our way to the appointment in Poughkeepsie. I'd heard the heartbeat. I'd seen movement. We'd gotten the blood work back; we knew the baby was a girl. I had ultrasound photos showing her growth. But I couldn't let myself enjoy it. During the high-risk ultrasound, they checked every single inch of the baby. They measured everything while I looked up at the screen showing our baby inside of me. You can see everything. Her profile, her little hands. The tech knew that we were scared and said, "She's perfect. If I were having a baby, this is the ultrasound I would want."

But I was so untrusting.

Then the doctor came in and said, "She's perfect. There's not even one yellow flag here."

"I knew it," Jeff said. "Awesome. Just awesome. Thank you, doc." And then he got real huggy with this man he had only just met. The doctor left the room, and Jeff saw my face. The terror of letting yourself feel joy after great loss can be overwhelming. My chin got tight as it does when I'm fighting emotion. He pulled me into his chest and whispered, "It's gonna be great."

All of a sudden we thought we should pick out a name, we should get ready for this little girl.

We sat in the backyard, watching Gus splash in the pool during one of those hot early autumn days. I'd written up long lists of girl names, combinations of names I liked from books and old family names. Jeff was polite about it, but I could tell they were all rather stuffy and old-fashioned for his liking. Anne—from *Anne of Green Gables*—was a front-runner. Virginia, an homage to my home. Liesel, Elise, and various other versions of my mother's name, Lisa. Dolley, derived from my fixation on Dolley Madison. But nothing was clicking.

"To hell with it. Let's just name her George," I said.

Jeff lit up. "I was gonna say that yesterday, but I thought you'd hate it!"

"I was gonna say it earlier, but I thought *you'd* hate it!"

To this day, I still have no idea how we separately and simultaneously arrived at the name George.

Later, while diving into my divine feminist studies, I looked up the area in Spain where I'd lit the votive candles in Barcelona. The patron saint? St. George.

Meanwhile, I hadn't communicated any of this to the wedding planner in St. Maarten. She kept asking me questions, and I kept putting her off, but she was holding our money and all of our friends' money and there was a no-returns policy. Our wedding was scheduled for January 4. The baby was due February 11, and while all of this was unfolding, the Zika virus had taken over the island. So once I had the ultrasound, I called the wedding planner and told her we had to cancel. "We'll do anything we can to help on social media to promote your venue, and you've got months to book the rooms, so is there any way we get our money back?"

When I hung up the phone, Jeff said, "I'm out a shit ton of money aren't I? And all our friends are out thousands of dollars."

I felt sick about it, but I had to send an email to all our friends. "There's good news and bad news. Good news is we're having a girl! Bad news is St. Maarten has Zika. We are so grateful that every single one of you was willing to celebrate our wedding with us. Jeff and I will absolutely cover any costs from the resort that won't be reimbursed." I groveled. I felt so horrible.

Without fail, everybody wrote back: baby trumps wedding.

But Jeff was still holding out hope. "Hilarie, we could make it work. I've looked into planes to crop dust the entire island of St. Maarten to kill the mosquitoes. We'll put you in a net; you'll be fine."

He so badly wanted this wedding. He had his heart set on it.

But I dug in. "Honey, we've tried so long to get pregnant, we aren't risking anything."

Don't get me wrong, I wanted to get married, and I was frustrated that we couldn't get our money back. But I would've paid hundreds of thousands of dollars for a baby. Millions. This baby was priceless. We agreed to go to the island and get married after our baby was born.

Then Hurricane Irma hit, and the island was decimated. The hotel was swept away, and all our intimate misfortunes were thrown into perspective. The hotel wrote to us to say that they would return everyone's money. They didn't exist anymore. I'd been so irritated with them, and now I was heartbroken for them. Life is about constantly changing perspective.

With the wedding canceled and the doctor's stamp of approval, I finally gave myself permission to daydream about my girl. I didn't want to deprive myself of joy because I was so scared of losing the baby. Pregnancy with Gus had been stressful because I was a first-time mom and Jeff was always gone, and there were so many logistical issues. So my pregnancy with our daughter was kind of a do-over. Now I had a home. I knew where Jeff was. Our life had a routine. I wanted to move forward and remove all the negative shit. I was very conscious of the fact that I was creating someone else's cells, I was creating the chemistry of her brain; so if my body was a cauldron of negativity and adrenaline and stress, then it would affect the baby. I devoted myself to serenity. No more *Dateline*. No more spinning wheels and anxiety. It was gonna be all sunshine and rainbows from that point on.

16

I wish I were a girl again,
half-savage and hardy, and free.

—**Emily Brontë, *Wuthering Heights***

I n October 2017 I was lying in bed live-tweeting during my episodes of *Lethal Weapon* when a tweet caught my eye from @ShaniceBrim, who was talking about Ben Affleck in the aftermath of the news about Harvey Weinstein: *He also grabbed Hilarie Burton's breast on TRL once. Everyone forgot though.*

My heart jumped. I couldn't believe that somebody else remembered that. It had been my own personal grievance, a distant memory that no one mentioned anymore. I felt something akin to shame, that another woman out there had spoken up on my behalf when I'd swept so much of my own shit under the rug so as to not cause a scene.

I didn't forget, I tweeted back.

@ShaniceBrim wrote me again: I'm so sorry that happened to you. It's infuriating that people never bring up all the gross, predatory things he's done.

Seriously, thank you for that. I was a kid, I wrote. Then I found the old video of the incident on the internet. I saw myself laughing and then saying, "Well, he played that card, huh. Ha ha." Then there was a video of me later saying, "Yeah, I would've preferred a high-five."

I sent @ShaniceBrim that video and said: I had to laugh back then so I wouldn't cry. Sending love.

I went to bed that night and thought nothing of it. But I woke up to a shit show, as all the #MeToo news shook out. I found myself watching old footage of a nineteen-year-old me trying so hard to laugh off the ugliness of being a girl. By the time the week of chaos and unwanted requests from every news outlet under the sun was over, I was drained. I'd worked in media just long enough to know that none of those outlets really cared about me; they cared about dragging a famous guy through the mud. I let the old footage speak for itself, staying silent and fuming that the real story—the bigger trauma of my years on *One Tree Hill*—was of interest to no one.

In my youth, being a "good sport" led me down a rabbit hole. I thought I could protect myself by just being "one of the guys," by laughing at the crude jokes, by sidestepping advances, and by being one of those loud, lippy girls who shrugs off pretty much anything.

So I was the loudest and rough around the edges, and I feigned an "I don't give a shit" attitude. But in the end I was a young girl who wanted approval and was assaulted anyway.

I never tried to tell the truth to the media after I left *One Tree Hill* because I believed it was a lost cause. And I was a coward. I had walked away from jobs I loved just to remove myself from toxic situations. I stopped auditioning. I abandoned my childhood dreams of being an actress because playing the game was simply not worth it to me.

I'm so sorry about the girls and young women who have come after me and been traumatized. I'm sorry it took me so long to join the chorus. I'm hopeful for a future when cowards like me will be the exception and not the rule. Because I will be damned if my daughter ever becomes a "good sport."

That whole confusing week, my daughter kicked and squirmed inside me, making her presence known. *She will be here soon. This shit has got to stop.*

The timing of all the chaos couldn't have been worse. I put my head down and got back to work. Animals. Gardens. The nursery. And our second Ghost Stories event. I met Sonia from Astor over at the venue for a walkthrough.

"You doing okay?" she asked me. It was a loaded question. Sonia works with the kids at Astor every day and knows when people are covering their true feelings, denying their vulnerability. Her eyes are twinkly and a tad mischievous, and she has a presence that feels like a warm hug.

"It's been . . . hard."

"You must be tired. Just know that because you spoke up, other girls and young women will feel like they can speak up too." I immediately thought of the girls at Astor—girls who deserved to have their truths and traumas heard and recognized. I couldn't encourage them to be brave and audacious if I wasn't willing to do that myself.

"When do you think everything about Mark will come out?" Sophia asked me about the creator of *One Tree Hill*, Mark Schwahn.

"Beats the hell out of me."

"But it's got to, right?"

It had to, but after all the Affleck business, I was weary of being labeled a troublemaker. Mark could be incredibly malicious, and I was afraid to be the one to strike first. But then, one of the writers on the show, whom I had never met, Audrey Wauchope, acknowledged the abusive environment of *One Tree Hill* through a series of tweets. A fan forwarded Audrey's tweets to Sophia, Joy Lenz, and me, asking, Hey girls, does any of this ring a bell?

I called Sophia. "Oh fuck, it's happening."

I knew that Mark had gone after the actresses, but I had no idea that there had been abuse in the writers' room. We publicly supported Audrey through Twitter. I cheered her on with Burn it down sis, a catchphrase that became a rallying cry for women who were now ready to name names. On *One Tree Hill*, Sophia had been the pretty one, Joy the talented one, and I the angry one. But now, I began to realize, we were *all* angry.

Sophia started a text thread with a large group of the women from the show. Each one of us would bring in another actress or crewmember whom we knew had been hurt by the toxicity of that production. At the suggestion of Daphne Zuniga, eighteen women from the show wrote a joint letter stating that we had all been negatively affected by Mark's abusive behavior. The letter was direct, polite, angry, but vague; it did not detail specific events. There would have been too many to recount anyway.

E! News wouldn't cover the story because Mark's current show, *The Royals*, was on the E! network. They had done multiple articles on Ben Affleck groping me for one second almost twenty years before, but when a multitude of women were coming forward about years of abuse from the showrunner whose series was on their network, not a peep.

Nothing was done. Mark Schwahn wasn't fired. Then, the women from *The Royals* wrote a letter, and the lead actress made a personal statement. He was put on probation. But the media didn't care—not without gory details.

Variety needed specifics that could be backed up. Our text chain of women from *One Tree Hill* was on fire. Many of us wanted to talk, to tell the full, unexpurgated truth, but that idea was as frightening as it was liberating. When our letter didn't get the traction it needed, I wrote to the group:

> You guys, we can't be vague. They want the shitty details;
> otherwise, they'll think we're being dramatic.

We knew some of us were going to have to bite the bullet. A series of responses followed:

> Yes.
> Let's do it.
> Talk to them Hilarie, and then I'll do it the next day.

So I spilled my guts to Daniel Holloway at *Variety*; I talked to him for five hours. Danneel Ackles bravely detailed her abuse. Daniel's horror listening to our story validated so much of what I'd felt. And worse had happened to other women. But when he tried to follow up with some of those others, they were reprimanded by their management firms, their publicists, and their agents and told that doing this was career suicide. Some of them called me in tears, saying, "I'm so sorry—I hope you don't think less of me."

I looked around at my life and thought, *If I never work on another show or film, I'll be okay.* Mischief Farm was in the middle of its full autumn display, similar to the way it had looked when we'd seen it for the first time. *This is real*, I thought. *This is who I am.*

The farm. Samuel's Sweet Shop. Astor. The community. My children. Jeffrey.

This is what matters.

There is a moment of absolute freedom when you realize that the things that used to scare you have no power over you anymore. I had the freedom to tell the truth.

My daughter had steeled me. I was a farmer. A shop owner. A soccer mom. A board member at Astor. I was finally a person that I sorta kinda liked, and all the creeps out there could go straight to hell.

By the end of the year, Mark Schwahn had been fired.

Oh, earth, you're too wonderful for
anybody to realize you.

—Thornton Wilder, *Our Town*

George was a hyperactive baby, even in the womb. For all my wishing that I could get pregnant, actually being pregnant was much harder than I remembered. I was also almost a decade older. But that girl jumped and kicked and danced with such fervor that Gus would watch my rolling belly in horror. "Is that normal?" he'd ask.

I was convinced she was coming early. I began having Braxton-Hicks contractions toward the end of January. Sharagim had helped me find a wonderful midwife who worked through the hospital, so just like when I had Gus, I would have all the safety nets of a hospital at my disposal but the personal empowerment of natural birth. Nancey Rosensweig, an Ivy League–educated midwife with children of her own, brought a great deal of compassion to my healthcare. We met in my home, where she nursed the whole of me and looked after my mental health and my worries about having a healthy baby. She gave great advice regarding Gus and how to keep him involved and a priority. She brought me food and natural homeopathic remedies to ease my aches and pains and heartburn. Oh Lord, never in my life had I experienced such heartburn.

As we neared February, she told me, "The head is very low. I can feel it."

"She's coming soon, right?"

"It seems that way." Shit. Jeff had killed himself over the past year, working crazy hours and coming home from Georgia every chance he got. It was a heroic show of endurance and commitment to our family and farm, but we'd decided that once George was born, he'd take some time off. That meant knocking out as much work as possible before her arrival. He was headed on a cruise for *The Walking Dead*, a convention that thousands of fans were attending partly based on the assurance that he would be there. Right after that he was booked for another convention on the other side of the planet in Australia. "Honey, I'll be home by the sixth," he told me. "Baby isn't coming till the eleventh."

"You know that's not written in stone, right?" I countered. "She could come any day! I can feel her head now!" I was antsy and worried. I wanted to move around like the cows do out in the field when they're getting ready to go into labor.

Throwing on my boots and an old military surplus coat, I walked the perimeter of the farm. I labored under my own weight and against the eight or so inches of snow I trudged through. It felt good. *Be like a cow* was my mantra.

Only this cow overdid it and twisted her ankle.

When Jeff came home from the cruise, we had to have a serious talk about the Australia trip. "Babe, she's coming early," I fretted. "I'm dilating already."

"But I'll be there and back days before the due date."

"I. Am. Freaking. Out." There was no other way to say it. I needed him. In the last days of what I knew would be my last pregnancy ever, I needed him to lie in bed with me and make me feel safe, and no other person on the planet could fill that role.

He stayed.

The weekend of the Australia trip flew by. I was having continual contractions, but nothing was kicking into high gear. My mother had come up weeks before, stocking the fridge and freezer with food. My dad had taken the week of the eleventh off work so he could drive up and be here for the birth. Each day, Gus, my parents, and Jeffrey sat around staring at me.

"Today?" They'd ask.

"Maybe."

This kid had been killing me. She clearly wanted out. But she was toying with me.

My mom's birthday, February 7, came and went. I was big as a house, but we took her to dinner at Le Petit Bistro in town. That place is the *Cheers* of Rhinebeck. Everyone we know goes there, so of course we ran into various friends, who all noted, "You haven't given birth yet?"

No. Not yet.

The eleventh came and went. Nancey continued to check me out. "She's still just hanging out. Very low. And you're still 2 centimeters dilated. I can't believe you can walk!"

I took a peek at the journal Gus had started keeping. Day after day he wrote the same thing: "Still Prignit." Yep, still pregnant.

The week dragged on. On Valentine's Day, Jeff presented me with beautiful amethyst earrings, a ring, and a necklace. I was dripping in our daughter's birthstone. Bruce over at the jewelry store had outdone himself. "It was gonna be a baby present," he said. "But she's taking her sweet time."

I was mortified. I'd been so convinced that our girl was coming early. She was clearly as bullheaded as her mother.

My dad was going to have to leave that weekend, and I was so sad at the idea of his missing George's birth. Lord knows he wanted nothing to do with the delivery room. But my dad loves his grand-babies, and a twelve-hour drive to the farm and back was nothing to him—but so very much to me.

Five days after my due date, I lay in bed with Gus and Jeff. In the quiet of the morning, the rising sun caught the snow on the ground and filled our bedroom with bright white light. My boys glowed. I turned to throw an arm over the both of them, and felt an odd sensation. Like I had to pee, but different.

Tossing off the covers, I stood up, took two steps, and my water broke.

"Oh my gosh!" I yelled. My water hadn't broken with Gus. This was alien territory. I grabbed towels and started cleaning up the mess, but every time I moved it just kept coming—like an oily saline solution. I was doused and needed help.

"You okay?" Jeff mumbled from bed.

"Um, I might need your help."

I called Nancey. "Are you having contractions?"

"Not yet."

"Okay. Meet me at 11 at the hospital, okay? I'll bring some ho-meopathic aides."

Jeffrey loaded my bag into the truck and drove my mother and me over to the Neugarten Family Birth Center at the hospital. It was a cheery space, dedicated to bringing life into the world. I marched in with a huge smile on my face. The ladies at reception said, "How can we help you today, ma'am?"

"I'm here to have a baby," I declared.

Far from the wide open pastures where our creatures just drop their babies in fields, the hospital had all sorts of implements to help get you through labor. Nancey set me rocking on a large exercise ball and had little homeopathic tablets that she told me to put on my tongue every so many minutes.

"Why? What is it?"

"They'll make your contractions successful."

I didn't know what that meant, but they kicked in very quickly. Every single contraction was doing a lot of work. I rocked and rocked and rocked, and when the rocking didn't help anymore, I moved over to the shower, where hot water pounded onto my lower back and I rocked standing up. *Be a cow.*

Jeffrey was in his Carhartt farming gear, snow boots, and a baseball cap. He played music with his phone that he knew our girl would like. I braced myself on his arm as Stevie Nicks and Journey powered through the speakers. Then something shifted deep down in my guts and I just knew. I yelled out, "She's coming!"

All hands on deck, I was led to the bed. Back at Christmastime my mother and sisters-in-law had conducted a blessing ceremony for my pregnancy, gifting me with a necklace they had made of various stones to empower me during delivery. My mother stood next to me holding it and patting my back. Focusing on those stones, I prepped myself to push. But Nancey coached me to avoid the pain I'd felt with Gus. "Let the contraction do its job. And then bear down in between the contractions to push her down the canal." Well that went against everything I'd ever heard, but I trusted her and listened. She held warm towels against me to protect my body and give it a point to push against.

"I'd like a time estimate!" I yelled. "How long do you think?" There was a clock directly across from me. It was 4:50 p.m.

"Soon," the nurse up by my head said.

"But like five minutes soon or thirty? I gotta know how to pace myself."

My mother looked over at her and said, "She's very goal oriented."

Nancey and the nurse took a look. "By 5 o'clock" the nurse said. Ten more minutes. I could do that.

Any woman who has ever had a baby will tell you that those last few minutes are outrageous. The thoughts racing through your mind are insane. *Why am I doing this without drugs? Who is this person inside of me? Did I put the clothes in the dryer?*

Jeffrey kept up the encouragement. "You're so pretty. You're doing so good babe!" This time he had fully committed to being down where the action was, excited to catch our daughter. At 4:58, I had the contraction that set our girl free—she gently popped her head out, and Jeff gasped as he took her into his hands.

Cradling her head, he kept saying, "She's so beautiful, mama. She's so, so beautiful." Then he brought her up to meet me. She was dark, with full lips and a head of thick black hair. She was perfect. After all those months, I could finally breathe.

My dad and Gus arrived to meet our new family member, and I was literally up and walking around minutes after giving birth. I felt no pain.

George arrived on February 16, five days past her due date. She shares a birthday with my brother Billy and with Meg, my manager.

Jeff left after a while to get me a proper dinner. He must have made a parade around Rhinebeck, because everyone in town knew George had arrived. He bought a huge bouquet at the grocery store and picked up sushi at Osaka, spreading the word. Everyone at Samuel's heard the good news. Bruce. Ed. Mari Bird. All our Astor friends. Other shop owners in town. The outpouring of support and congratulations from this community of people who had allowed us in moved me.

After I gave birth to Gus, I'd been so lonely. All these years later, to bring a child into this circle of warmth and kindness was everything I had ever wanted. A snowstorm kicked up, guests left our room, and Jeffrey settled in to sleep in a reclining chair. In the wee hours of the morning, a young nurse started her rotation.

"How are you feeling?" she asked.

"You know what? It's weird. I feel perfectly fine. Like I didn't even have a baby." It was true. There was no swelling. No pain. I felt perfectly normal for the first time in months.

"Did you have Nancey?" she asked.

I nodded. "How'd you know?"

"Her nickname around here is the Vagina Whisperer. She's the best."

The Vagina Whisperer? Nancey had been underselling herself. She needed to lead with that in her sales pitch! She's certainly earned the moniker.

George was a power baby. From the moment she was born, she held her head up. Everyone commented on it, asking, "Is she old enough to be doing that?"

"She's a product of the Me Too movement," I'd say, half kidding. But as brassy or tough as I ever thought I was, my daughter showed me up. She took to alligator rolling, showing off her strength at an early age. She'd grab her sweet brother with such a tight grip, he wouldn't quite know what to do.

Our second Astor renovation was scheduled to happen a month after George was born. With her attached to me in her carrier, we created magic with the same team we'd worked with before. Every single one of them had shown back up, inspired by the kids.

The boys in the unit were ecstatic. They made me paintings and thank-you cards and all worked together to make a big card to welcome George into the world. As we revealed the space to them, all their barriers disappeared. They came up to George and examined her little hands and chubby cheeks. I was so grateful to everyone at Astor for helping see Jeffrey and me through this journey.

Spring came early. The next thing we knew, the farm had gone into full effect. The creeks were flooded with melting snow, and the flowers were pushing themselves up. Jeff was headed to a press tour for his film *Rampage*, and he knew he was going to be asked about George. He texted me from the airport.

I'm scared I'm gonna slip up and say the wrong thing.

I knew what he was feeling. When I was pregnant and we were trying to keep everything very hush hush, he'd been on a panel at a convention where he accidentally used the pronoun "she" when referring to the baby, and the entire crowd gasped. He dropped the mic and covered his face with his hands. Moments later he called me. "Babe, I messed up." I wasn't mad; I thought it was funny. News outlets ran the story: "Jeffrey Dean Morgan Accidentally Reveals Baby's Gender!"

He didn't want to make another mistake, and I appreciated the concern. How people would find out about George had been weighing heavily on my mind. All those years of loss and failure and pain had been compounded by the constant barrage of celebrity babies. The capitalization of this holy moment hurt me deeply as a woman who had difficulty staying pregnant. I was jealous of the women who found it so easy that they could put it all out there for the whole world to see.

"Let me write something, okay?"

"I think that's our best bet," he said.

It took me a while. George lay in my lap, lips all smooshed up and arms dangling off my leg. She was real. She had weight. She brought out the best in me and her dad and her brother. She made us laugh. She wore us out. I wanted to celebrate her, but not at the expense of another woman's heartache. I sent Jeffrey a draft of the letter.

> As some of you know, @jeffreydeanmorgan is off in Europe getting ready to do some big conventions. And he's self-aware enough to know that his track record for "spilling the beans" isn't so great (bless his heart!). So before he starts tripping up in an attempt to

maintain our privacy, he asked that I go ahead and post something about our little girl's birth.

But before I do that, there's something I really want to say to all the women out there who are trying . . .

It took a long time for Jeffrey and me to have this baby. The first time I got pregnant, it took a year and a half. I surprised him on Christmas with baby Seahawk booties. We cried. We celebrated. We picked out names. And we lost that baby.

More losses followed, and as so many couples know, it was heartbreaking. It still is heartbreaking.

And every morning of the five years it took us, I'd open my computer at the kitchen table and see the news and I'd grow bitter over the endless parade of celebrities showing off their bumps and babies. I'd weep out of jealousy for how easy it was for them. Didn't they know something could go wrong? Didn't they know that there were other women out there struggling? It pained me to see the corporate-sponsored baby showers and magazine covers capitalizing on this human miracle that wasn't happening for us.

So when this pregnancy started, we were cautious. I didn't want to celebrate for fear of jinxing it. I didn't want a baby shower. I checked her heartbeat every day, up until the day she was born. And now that she is here, I just stare at her in wonder all day. I see her in her daddy's arms and I don't take any of it for granted. She screams bloody murder and I smile because she is so wildly alive.

So now that folks know she's here, I don't want her birth to cause any other woman to weep at her kitchen table. If anything, my wish is that she would restore hope for others. Fertility is a fickle thing. And for the other couples out there who have had dark days, we want to introduce our miracle baby to you and send you our love and support in finding yours.

Please meet George Virginia Morgan. She was born February 16th. Her daddy delivered her. We love her very much.

"Ah babe," he responded. "I'm crying. It's a lot to share. But yes. Post that. I love you."

I sent the message out into the ether, not quite knowing what to expect.

The avalanche of compassion and women confessing their own struggles completely caught me off guard. Thousands and thousands of broken hearts reached out, each with their own stories. I cried as I read their responses, hoping they, too, would find something to share their love with—whether it be a baby or a labor of love like Astor, or a town like Rhinebeck. Or a place like Mischief Farm.

I hadn't dyed my hair in ages, and looking in the mirror I was confronted by a sea of gray. The previous ten years had changed me, aged me, prepared me.

Mischief Farm had been the game changer. We'd tell people where we lived and they'd say things like, "Oh, that's our retirement dream," or "We wanna do that someday." But with all of the loss we'd known, I wanted to scream, *No! Do it now. Don't you realize we only get one chance?* New people we met assumed that Jeff and I could handle this lifestyle because we came from agricultural upbringings. *No! We just wanted it, so we reinvented ourselves. I'm not a farmer. I'm a Burton. We're liars.*

It was true. If we could pull this off, anyone could.

"I think we should share the farm with people," I said to Jeff one day while George rocked in her swing.

"Like how?"

"Like all the things we've discovered that we love about this place. The plants we love. The honey. The local artisans. Your knives and axes. We love those things. We should share them." We pulled out a scrap of paper. Going all the way back to our *Lonesome Dove* beginnings, Jeff started fiddling with the idea of a cattle brand. To share the farm, we needed a logo. Something edgy enough for him but wholesome enough for me. We settled on a combined *M* and *F* with a circle around it.

MF. Mother Fucker for my dearest. Mama Farmer for me.

And Mischief Farm for everyone else.

All the lessons we'd gathered from living here, from buying Samuel's, from engaging with our neighbors and celebrating their talents—we wanted to share that.

The same way I had been inspired by other people's stories when I was low, I wanted to pay it forward and continue the message: *Try. The want-to creates the how-to. And if all else fails, just fake it. But for God's sake, at least try.*

Our anniversary rolled up again in early May. Jeff was home, and, with George attached to me in her carrier and Gus running ahead, we took a family stroll down to the barn. Paxton jumped all over Jeffrey, Gus started his new favorite chore of brushing the girls, and Princess came up to inspect the baby. I hadn't been down to the barn in a long while. My pregnancy had been a paranoid one, and I hadn't wanted to take any chances. Gus brushed and brushed Ally, and I started really looking at her. "Jeff, she's super fat."

"Yeah, she's not doing so good, but I don't know how to keep her from eating. You know, she's in a field all day, you can't really do portion control."

Then I got a good look at her from behind, and it dawned on me that she was 100 percent pregnant. Donkeys have an eleven-month pregnancy, and I'd gotten these donkeys exactly eleven months earlier. This girl must have gotten pregnant the day before we got her, and we just thought she was a fatty!

"No," Jeff insisted. "She's just a chub."

The next day I ran out to the supermarket. No baby. I pulled back up the drive and peered in the pasture as I drove by.

BABY!!!

Jeff came tearing out of the house, yelling "No way!" Some farmers we were!

We looked the baby over and brought Gus down to see it. "Is it a boy or girl?" he wanted to know. Jeff bent his head this way and that, trying to get a closer look.

"I think it's a girl," he said. I seconded the motion.

We named her Loretta.

Weeks later we discovered *she* was really a *he*. So now we have a daughter with a boy name, and a little boy donkey with a girl name. Clearly, anything is possible at Mischief Farm.

For every death, there is a birth. For every winter, there is a summer. And as things bloom and grow and live here, we are constantly reminded what a gift it is to put our hands in the dirt and connect with the land and each other through Mischief Farm.

ACKNOWLEDGMENTS

There's always the fear that you will forget someone when saying thank you. So please let me begin by saying that I'm so grateful to every single person in this book. As I said in the beginning, this is a love letter. My affection runs deep for all the people, places, and creatures in its pages. Happiness begins with gratitude, and so I humbly thank all the folks who have contributed to my family's joy. Now that that's established, let's commence with the love fest.

Alexis Gargagliano—I've been writing my entire life, but there was so much I needed to be taught. Thank you for being a supportive teammate and a wealth of knowledge and patience. I respect the hell out of you.

Meg Mortimer—since I was nineteen years old, you have been my rock. Thank you for always defending me and never pushing me to be anything other than myself. I love you very, very much. Your husband and kids are pretty damn great too!

Rick Dorfman, Liz DeCesare, and Anthony Mattero—thank you for believing in me and supporting me in the creation of this project. You were the first to see the vision.

Katy Hamilton and the HarperOne family—thank you for hearing my story and absolutely getting what I wanted to say with this book. You are true champions, and I hope we continue to create together.

The amazing team that supports Jeffrey and me: Robert Strent, Jordan Manekin, Barry McPherson, Abe Altman, Jeanne Yang,

Theresa Peters, Jen Allen, Sara Planco, and Stuart Rosenthal—you all easily could have given us hell for running away and falling off the radar. Instead, you put our happiness over any work concerns and supported us at every turn. I'm so thankful.

Big shout-out to Steve Pregiato and Jeffrey Robertson for guiding us through all of our stages—you two are so wonderful.

Danneel and Jensen Ackles—my God I love you guys. Thank you for knowing what I needed, even when I didn't.

Claudia, Doris, and Brittany—thank you for loving my children and helping me to be a better mother. We treasure the time you have spent with our family.

The late Deborah Frank, who showed me immeasurable kindness, Nancey Rosensweig, and the Neugarten Family Birth Center—as a woman who wanted to "get back to nature," I felt that the empowerment you gave me transcended childbirth.

Our various TV and film families: MTV, *One Tree Hill*, *White Collar*, *Lethal Weapon*, *Grey's Anatomy*, *Magic City*, *The Walking Dead*, my Christmas movie cult, and so many others—your enthusiasm for our lifestyle really made all the difference. Thank you for seeing the magic in it and for going out of your way to accommodate our special circumstances.

The Squatches: Ashley Hoyt, Erica Wible, Tory Silvestri, and Sarah Baughman—it would be impossible for me to love you more. Happiness is making movies in the Barnes basement and pool parties at the Dawsons.

Nick Gray—my soul twin. Let's make all the same mistakes together. Forever.

To the folks who welcomed us with open arms here in the Hudson Valley: Rick Reilly, our lovely neighbors on West Pine Road,

Roger and Pam Hoffman and the Barn Sale family, Ms. Patty, the Page family, Griffin Dunne and Charlie Wessler, Andrew Stewart and Cricket Lengyel, all the parents from school who have been exceedingly warm and inclusive—you don't know what it means to us as a family to have found this place. It truly takes a village. And ours is spectacular.

Jeremy and Addie Sisto—your validation of our little cabin in the woods started this whole full-time adventure. Move here already!

Andy and Sophie Ostroy, Phoebe Jonas, Julie, Paul, Jack, and Darby Rudd—you are our family. Our lives are infinitely richer for knowing you. Let's celebrate with an ice cream pie from Holy Cow!

John, Ally, and Charlie Traver—the bravery you showed after Ira's passing was so noble. Let's keep showering the world with sugar and caffeine forever! Love you guys.

To the businesses in town that started off as friendships and evolved into partnerships after our Samuel's purchase and during our work with Astor: Jeanne Fleming of Sinterklaas fame, Kim Williams and the Williams Lumber family, Barbara and Dick Schreiber of the Rhinebeck Department Store, Jass Liu and John Kim and family at Osaka, Connie and the gang at Pete's Famous Restaurant, Oblong Books & Music, Hammertown, Changes, Paper Trail, Land of Oz Toys, Liberty, Aroi, Piper Woods at Montgomery Row, Jen and Joe Dalu at Le Petite Bistro, Doug and Lynn at the Rhinebeck Artist's Shop, Joe and Kim Curthoys at Rhinebeck Wine and Liquor, Bruce and Jamie at Hummingbird Jewelers, Elena at Land of Oz Toys, my sweet sweet Mari Bird at Willow Wood, Davis Furniture in Poughkeepsie, the Rhinebeck Chamber of Commerce, the Town Board of Rhinebeck, Enjoy Rhinebeck, and too many others to mention—you have built an environment that is inspiring to be a part of. I hope this book serves as a testament to my gratitude.

Our Samuel's Sweet Shop team: Joan and Bill Burhans, John Marvin, Patricia Curthoys, David Tellerday at M&T Bank, Celeste Oxendine, Donna Weber, and all our other talented makers, our fabulous employees, and our loyal customers over the years—our little shop is a landmark of love, and it wouldn't exist without you.

Our Mischief Farm gurus: Sunny, Dana and family, Ed and Barb Hackett and their wonderful kids, all the folks at Hackett Farm Supply, the Whalens, our vets Gillian Ferguson and Countryside Animal Hospital, Dr. Crumb, Twist of Fate Spinnery, and all the other hardworking men and women who have been so generous with their knowledge and time—we will always be a work in progress, so your belief in us and your friendships have been such blessings. Thank you.

Our dear friends Sharagim and Sean Kemp and Tara Shafer and Gavin Curran—you have been there through the good, the bad, and the ugly. It's crazy how life works, putting you exactly where you need to be at any given time. And I'm so glad I was put here with you. I love you and your families madly.

Astor and all the wonderful people who came into my life because of it: Kate and Mike Kortbus, Lawrie and Bryan Firestone, Donna Faraldi, Jim and Ginny Schwab along with Families for Astor, Sonia Barnes-Moorhead, Jim McGuirk, Kim McGrath, James Reardon, Ed Pruitt and the amazing staff at our Rhinebeck facility, Mark and Jess McEathron and the whole team of McEathron Contracting, Chuck Merrihew, Mike Sr. and Mike Jr. of Stanhope

Electric, Mike Diblasi and the family of Diblasi Painting, Tim Decker, Frank Talbot, Rob Hunter from Benjamin Moore, Mary Stuart Masterson, Clayne Crawford, Michael Raymond James, Tyler Hilton, and all of our other talented friends who have helped us at our fundraising performance each year, and all the members of the press who have lovingly covered our efforts—thank God for you. Honestly. You spread light and love, and I'm humbled to work alongside you.

To the families and loved ones of Sgt. Scott Kirkpatrick, Ira Gutner, and Bill Paxton—thank you. Thank you for sharing your guys with us. Thank you for letting us claim a tiny bit of their memory. Thank you for loving them and helping to create such warm, smart, generous spirits. In our lives, we all hope to make a difference and leave something valuable behind. Scott and Ira and Bill are imprinted on our hearts, and they are the legends we tell our kids about. Sending you all so much love and gratitude.

To Jeff's parents, Dick and Kath Morgan and Sandy and Tom Thomas—I love your son. Thank you for him, and for celebrating the crazy turn our lives took when we moved here.

To my mom and dad, Bill and Lisa Burton—weekend trips to Skyline Drive, Christmas tree shopping, making homemade Halloween costumes, telling stories that we'd repeat over and over—you made magic out of the mundane. If I have accomplished anything of value in my life, it is because you believed in me and gave me the tools to take risks. I love you.

My brothers and their spouses: Billy, John, Conrad, Kim, Christina, Jessica—planting pumpkins behind the house, telling secrets through the vents, jumping off of the top bunk, ghost encounters and belief in Bigfoot—we are a tribe of weirdoes, and

I cherish all of our shared adventures. Love you guys. Otto and Rhett Burton! Auntie Hil is obsessed with you wild men!

Jeffrey Dean. My husband—you work harder, love stronger, and have more faith in me than anyone. When I am a hundred years old, rocking in my chair, lost in memories, I will replay our story over and over and smile for all the joy we have had. Thank you for finding me.

Augustus Dean and George Virginia—there is no accomplishment in my life greater than being your mother. It is what I've wanted my entire life. I love the life we have built here, but I'm keenly aware that home is wherever you two are. I love our winters in front of the fire. I love our springs playing in the flowers. I love our summers getting dirty in the garden. And I love our autumns with their colorful festivities. You two are golden and the whole heart of Mischief Farm.

Mama adores you.

And thank YOU for reading this book and supporting Mischief Farm. Shop at mom-and-pop establishments and support local farmers as much as you can. They are the tapestry that makes our small towns so very beautiful.

ABOUT THE AUTHOR

Hilarie Burton Morgan has been a grocery store checkout girl, a waitress, an MTV VJ, an actress, a farmer, a candy store owner, a producer, and is now an author. But she is proudest to be a mother and wife. She lives with her husband and two wild children in the Hudson Valley of New York.